Whole Language Evaluation for Classrooms
©1992 Orin and Donna Cochrane

Published in the United States in 1992 by
The Wright Group
19201 120th Avenue NE
Bothell, WA 98011-9512

First published in Canada in 1992 by
Whole Language Consultants Ltd.
#6-846 Marion Street
Winnipeg, Manitoba
Canada
R2J 0K4

Printed in Canada
10 9 8 7 6 5 4 3 2 1

ISBN: 0-7802-0657-6

WHOLE LANGUAGE
EVALUATION
FOR CLASSROOMS

ISBN 0-921253-22-2
PRINTED IN CANADA

Published in Canada in 1992 by
    Whole Language Consultants Ltd.
    #6-846 Marion Street
    Winnipeg, Manitoba
    Canada
    R2J 0K4

WHOLE LANGUAGE EVALUATION FOR CLASSROOMS

Orin and Donna
Cochrane

v

Index

Introduction

Learning to Talk the Same Language

What is the definition of "reading?" At the end of this sentence, stop reading for a moment and write down in one or two sentences what you believe reading is. Probably, if ten teachers each wrote their personal definitions of reading, we would have at least three or four differing definitions. Some teachers might not even want to or be able to define reading. But if you cannot define reading, how will you know how to teach children to read? What you believe to be true about reading will be reflected in the manner in which your students process print, whether they construct meaningful text or "bark at print" and neglect meaning.

The best definition of reading I have seen is that "reading is thought stimulated by print for the purpose of constructing a meaningful text."

Much of what whole language evaluation can do is give teachers a common vocabulary for talking about children's learning. With a common vocabulary, we can measure similar aspects about reading with similar instruments or types of observations. Observations and instruments will be similar from classroom to classroom but not exactly the same. Each teacher needs to construct his/her own evaluation system, which will be unique to his/her particular class and community.

The instrument of evaluation and the types of observations employed in evaluation need to match our definitions of reading. Today's standardized tests, with filling in the blanks, underlining, circling, or any other activity that fragments language, cannot measure reading where the definition sees children *constructing* their own meaning of text according to their individual purposes and prior experiences. Standardized evaluations are bad simply because they do not meet anyone's definition of what reading really is.

EVALUATION PROCESS

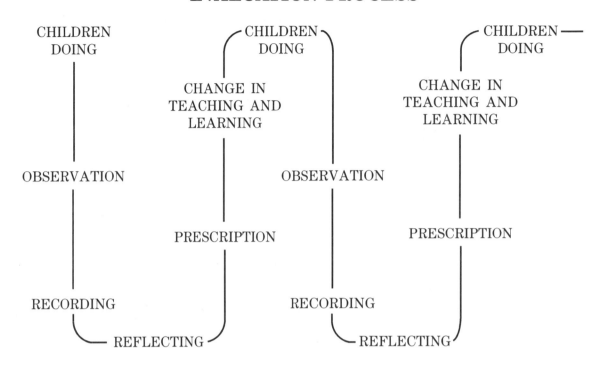

Evaluation as a Process

Whole language evaluation is best seen as a cyclical process based on observing individual students. The steps in this process are as follows.

1. *Doing* - Evaluation is rooted in the actions of the child as he/she strives to meet his/her needs. Teachers need to base their evaluations on skillfully observing students engaged in activities. Evaluation of only a written test paper is never sufficient.

2. *Observation* - Our evaluation comes from observing the child as he/she is involved in a task or a series of tasks. At times, the child's environment will be specifically structured to allow us to observe his/her reaction to a specific situation. For example, Vygotsky (a Russian psychologist who helped provide a theoretical base that whole language is based on) found that when he put an obstacle in the way of a young child who was

performing a routine task that the amount of egocentric talk increased. From these observations Vygotsky concluded that the child was using oral language as a tool to help work through the problem. Structuring of an environment to observe student response can be called a test. Formal paper and pencil tests are often a radical restructuring of the child's environment.

3. *Recording Data* - We record the actions and language of children as they endeavor to solve problems in structured situations. To whole language teachers, it is as important to record *how* the problem is solved by the child as well as his/her solution to the problem.

4. *Reflection* - It is also important that the child's solution to the problem be seen in the overall context of the situation, i.e. what prior experience the child brings to the solution and the social situation that influenced the setting of the problem. The social situation means the attitudes of the people in the environment the attitude of the teacher, the child, parents, and peers toward learning and solving problems. The important point is that whole language teachers see the testing situation in the whole context of the child's learning and that they reflect upon how the testing data fits in with all they know about the child.

5. *Prescription* - Now for the heart of the matter. Evaluation that stops at the point of reflection is dead evaluation leading nowhere. What we as whole language teachers must do is let our reflection on the child in the testing situation lead to a diagnosis of what the child is presently able to do behaviorally and cognitively and have that diagnosis lead to a prescription for the next step in the child's learning.

6. *Change in Teaching and Learning* - Our prescription will be the ways in which we will alter the child's learning environment so that he/she can continue to learn and progress to the

next stage of learning. We, as teachers, do this by making the child's learning environment rich in the demonstrations of the process of what the child is trying to learn. We alter materials, teaching strategies, teacher talk, and peer interaction to draw the child's attention to demonstrations of what he/she is striving to learn.

7. *Doing* - We give the children ample opportunities to attempt the activities that will aid their learning, focusing on what they themselves are purposefully trying to learn.

8. We continue the cycle by observing the children's progressive approximations toward the standard.

Traditional standardized evaluation is dead. It begins not with the living child but with preordained percentiles, stanines, or other boxes into which children are sorted. Traditional evaluation structures the child's environment into an artificial test situation unrelated to or, at best, semi-related to the background of real experiences the child brings to that situation. The child's responses are recorded, but the process by which the responses are generated is ignored. The only reflection upon the responses is to grade the paper and place the child in one of the preordained boxes. And that is the end of it, no diagnosis, no prescription, no altering of educational environment to meet the needs of the child. The culmination of traditional standardized evaluation is only a label for the child to live up to, or as often, down to. Any altered educational environment will not be to meet the child's individual educational needs, but rather to place him/her in a group program or keep him/her out of a more enriched group program, that is the fatal flaw of traditional evaluation; its lack of process, not being rooted in the child's individual previous learning, and not leading to new and altered individual learning circumstances.

Whole language evaluation is alive and empowers the teachers who practice it and the children who grow with it. It is not the opposite of standard evaluation; it is totally different in concept and practice.

Evaluation

Teachers who teach from a whole language perspective are often confronted with the rather difficult question "How do you evaluate the progress of the students you work with?" This question tends to be a very personal question to teachers of whole language because the curriculum is individualized to each student and to the particular class. Prior to whole language, the question of evaluation was not directed as much to the individual classroom teacher but more to curriculum writers, publishing companies, and test developers.

Teachers in whole language classrooms are acutely aware of the necessity of evaluating their students' progress and also of being able to articulate in a coherent manner exactly what their evaluation practices are. In this book, we will attempt to validate and extend the evaluation practices teachers in whole language classrooms are using.

Why Evaluate?

1. *We evaluate in order to make educational decisions.* We make decisions that determine the learning direction of our students. Teachers need to know what their students already know in order to develop units of work that fit the class and each student in it. Units of work that are developed without this knowledge tend to be too easy for some students and too difficult for others, as a result, these students begin to tune out or display disruptive behavior. As teachers we need to continually have evaluation procedures that will help us set a learning environment that will be as close as possible to the learning level of each of our students.

2. *We evaluate to determine growth.* We are moving away from measuring a student's learning by comparing one student to

another toward comparing the student's present learning to his/her past achievements. In whole language evaluation, emphasis is put on determining the amount of growth the student has achieved over a period of time. This is a highly individualized approach to evaluation and requires the teacher to collect such things as dated work samples, observations and taped oral readings to base the assessments on. As whole language teachers we want to be able to determine the direction of the child's language growth as it moves by progressive approximations toward standard form.

3. *We evaluate to communicate and share information about language growth to parents and other educators.* Parents want to know if their child is growing in his/her language competence. They want to know *what* activities their child has been engaged in and if they have been effective in promoting language growth. To validate the evaluation, the dated work samples, taped oral readings, bulk reading records and reading development assessments must be available.

The Roots of Whole Language Evaluation

In order for us to keep the *value* in our evaluation, it is necessary that our practices be rooted in whole language theory and principles.

In evaluating the child's progress in whole language the following principles must be adhered to:

1. *Evaluation must take place in a variety of meaningful and purposeful language situations.* That is, the language being evaluated must be authentic language used in real language situations. It is in situations where language is used as the tool it is meant to be that evaluation has meaning.

Evaluation then takes on a very broad form. The teacher bases his/her observations of the child's use of language in many situations in order that the conclusions drawn will be comprehensive. No longer is one test or one observation considered to be indicative of the student's learning.

2. *Learning must be viewed as developmental.* Language learning, like any other learning, is developmental. Besides evaluating the language in meaningful and purposeful situations, the evaluator must hold a developmental view of learning. Whole language teachers understand that learning is a series of approximations toward the standard. Therefore the teacher early in the year, begins to keep records of the observations of the child's use of language. Evaluation then become a continuous and ongoing process as opposed to tests and measures administered once or twice a term before reporting to parents. Dated work samples and dated observations are kept in order to determine the growth pattern. Teacher-made tests administered once or twice in a term may be a small part of the evaluation package but certainly not the entire evaluation package.

3. *There must be a positive view of the student's learning.* Teachers must constantly search for the strengths the child brings to the learning process and the strengths that the new learning exhibits. Whole language philosophy is built on a cognitive view of learning in which the learner's prior experiences are viewed as the basic building blocks for future learning. In the past, we have looked for what the child didn't know and taught these concepts and we were often left wondering why the child didn't learn very effectively. When new learning is based on what the child already knows, it becomes easy. The learner is motivated by successful experiences and becomes more and more confident as a learner and more readily approaches challenging tasks. When evaluation is based on the strengths of the learner, evalu-

ation becomes individualized and the curriculum becomes child-centered and meaningful.

4. *Process and product are both considered for evaluation.* Product has always had, and still has, an important place in evaluation. We must continue to evaluate the product, but not without evaluating the process as well. It is only through observing and reflecting on how the child produced the product that we will be able to address excellence in product.

5. *The quality of the miscue is more important than the quantity.* In the past, a child was given a number or a letter grade to indicate the child's knowledge. A mark of 87% or a B on a reading test doesn't tell the student or the teacher anything about the strengths or the weaknesses of the child's learning. It doesn't reveal anything about the child's thinking process. In whole language evaluation, we are interested in observing a child's miscues in a qualitative way. We ask ourselves such questions as "Does this miscue alter the sense of the passage?" and/or "Does it sound like language?" As teachers, we want to know 'why' the student miscued in the way he/she did. A mark denoting twenty-five miscues or mistakes tells us nothing about the child's use of language. It is only by carefully looking at the miscues that we gain insights about how a student is using the reading process, and what his/her strengths and needs are.

6. *The whole child has to be considered in the evaluation.* An evaluation that omits looking at the whole child will be remiss. We have to consider the child's home culture and language because this often has a big impact on the kind of learning a child is engaged in. We have to consider the history of the classroom. We have to consider the child's intent and his/her willingness to take a chance on learning. These are just some of the factors

that affect the child's learning and must be considered in the evaluation process.

Who Should Be Involved in the Evaluation Process?

Traditionally, the teacher was responsible for the evaluation of the student's progress with little or no input from parent(s) or the student. A report was given, and although it was discussed, there was very little opportunity for influence by either the student or the parent(s) on the report. In whole language evaluation, we see that the teacher, the student, and the parent(s) have critical roles in the process. By all three parties working collaboratively to determine progress and future learning, a true sense of community develops, and the student is the winner.

Reading Evaluation

What teachers believe to be true about reading will affect how their students use the reading process.

What teachers believe about "valuing" the child will affect their "evaluation" of children.

The Reading Development Continuum

Please take the time to become familiar with the Reading Development Continuum. It provides a common vocabulary for talking about a child's development in reading. Without this common vocabulary, we often find ourselves using the same words but not sharing the same meaning. For example, "What is a beginning reader?" I am sure that if we ask five teachers that question we would come up with six differing definitions of "a beginning reader." Ask five teachers who understand the Reading Development Continuum, "What is a Bridger?" and they will all tell you that it is a child who is beginning to realize that print plays an important role in reading. He/she already knows about the syntax and semantics of stories but is not yet able to use these cuing systems in a process of predicting, confirming, disconfirming and building a story meaning for the print. These teachers will be able to recommend appropriate strategies for this reader — strategies that will draw the child's attention to the print and lead him/her toward the efficient use of the reading process. These teachers will be able also to place the child on the continuum after only five minutes of working with him/her. The Reading Development Continuum is a powerful tool because:

a) it creates a common vocabulary for teachers,
b) it helps a teacher prescribe strategies that will be appropriate to a child's place in the development of reading,
c) the placement procedure is relatively quick.

Developing the Continuum

"What is a beginning reader?" was a question that lead a number of Winnipeg educators to look carefully at how reading develops. Many of us had young children at home and taught in elementary schools, so we were able to observe closely what children were doing at home and at school as their abilities to use reading developed, from the time they were born until the teen years. Our observations became the Reading Development Continuum stages.

Magical Stage

When a child is born he/she, seems to view a book like any other object. He/she may chew it, or throw it, or pull it apart. Very quickly, however, the child begins to see that a book has a purpose. People read to him/her, and he/she will listen contentedly for longer and longer periods of time. Familiar readings are usually listened to longer than unfamiliar ones. The children begin to see that pages of books are turned from the front to the back of the books. They see that we start at the top of a page and go down. They begin to see that reading "tells a story" or has a meaning. They will carry books to an adult to read to them. At this stage, the children do not attempt to read. The ability to provide meaning from print is outside of themselves. It is "magically" provided by an older person who reads to him/her. In households where there are books and a child is read to regularly, the magical stage lasts till the child is about three years old. In cases where the child is not exposed to books and not read to regularly, he/she may still be at a magical stage at five years old when he/she comes to school. *It is in the magical stage that the child is learning "book handling skills" and the purpose of books.*

Self-Concepting Stage

When our children were about three years old, we began to notice them doing things like sitting in chairs with their pet cat and "reading" to it. What they read to the cat sounded like a story and made sense. They might have begun with "story language" such as "Once upon a time," and what they "read" sounded like a real story. The story, however, only loosely corresponded to the printed text of the book. These children viewed themselves as readers and engaged in reading-like behaviors. The term "self-concepting themselves as readers" is a Don Holdaway term. It is during this "self-concepting stage" that these children were concentrating on the semantic and syntactic cuing systems of reading. The grapho-phonemic system was not in place. *That is, what they "read" to the cat made sense and sounded like book language but was not yet stimulated by the child interacting with print.*

Bridging Stage

It is at this time that the child begins to become aware that print plays an important role in reading. The child begins to notice letters and familiar words; for example, his/her own name and special words such as "the end." Key words, as outlined by Sylvia Ashton Warner, can excite the child's interest in this stage of reading development. By the time the child is fully into this stage, he/she will be able to find individual words in familiar print and tell you the letter that the word starts with. By the end of the stage, the child will be be able to "read" familiar passages that he/she is not able to completely recite from memory. *The child is now learning about the visual aspect of reading; that print makes a difference.*

Take-Off Stage

Bill Martin Jr. has said, "A child learns to read in six weeks." When he said this, he was referring to the next stage in reading development, the take-off stage, when the child begins to use the process of reading. The child learns to:

a) predict the meaning of the print based on his/her own prior experiences with print,

b) confirm or disconfirm those predictions,

c) build or construct a story meaning for the text. *The child can now read familiar print in new settings.* For example, if he/she has read

> Happy Birthday to you,
> Happy Birthday to you,
> Happy Birthday, dear Noodles,
> Happy Birthday to you.

and he/she is shown new print that reads, "Did you have a happy birthday Billy?" and he/she reads the unfamiliar text, he/she has reached the take-off stage of reading development.

At this time, it is vital to remember Frank Smith's sage advice: "The way to make the learning to read easier is to make the reading easier. The way to make the reading easier is to make it more predictable. The way to make it more predictable is to make it make sense and to sound like real language." It must make sense and sound like language in terms of what the child already knows about literacy and language.

N.B. At this stage, children need to read to a skilled reader every day. Their excitement in their accomplishment of moving toward becoming an independent reader will be obvious to all. This moment brings joy to a teacher's heart.

Independent Stage

At this point, the child

a) knows book handling skills, from the magical stage,

b) knows the role of the nonvisual cuing systems of syntax and semantics, from the self-concepting stage;

c) knows the role of the grapho-phonemic and/or the visual array cuing systems from the bridging stage, and

d) knows how to use the reading process of predicting, confirming or disconfirming, and integrating this into his/her view of the story from the take-off stage.

The child can now independently read a small book that he/she has not seen before. As an independent reader, the child needs to spend lots of time of practicing his/her newly found skill. He/she does this with great pleasure, as the child who has just learned to ride a bike, rides it for sheer pleasure. Learning is a joyful process. It is its own reward. Tokens or candies are not necessary.

Skilled Stage

Eventually, children no longer ride bikes just to ride bikes. They ride them for a purpose, such as to go to a friend's house, to deliver papers, or to win a race. So, too, readers will begin to read for a purpose. They will read to get done the things they need to have done in their lives.

Purposes for Reading (Functions of reading)

There are many things we accomplish in our life through reading. These things can be categorized in many ways. The continuum categorizes purposeful reading into four areas.

1. *Reading for information.* This is reading to find out what to do or how to do something or to find an answer to a question.

2. *Reading for entertainment.* This is reading for enjoyment, such as reading comics or the sports pages. It can be reading to pass the time, as in a dentist office when we read an article on tartar control while we wait for the inevitable drill or as on an airplane when we read those airline magazines.

3. *Reading to Read.* We, who are readers, must at times just get lost in a book. We must partake of the experience of reading a novel and be vicariously transported to another world, another life. Many teachers just wait for July when they can get lost in a novel and dwell in the land of reading. It is easy

to tell if children read for this purpose. Just ask children if they have read for more than thirty minutes continuously over the summer holidays.

4. *Maintenance of Self.* An example of this is when we might read in Ukrainian to maintain our ancestral heritage. We may read professional journals to keep our "teacherness." Or we may read about chess to remain the class "chess expert." Reading can maintain who we think we are and who others perceive us to be.

To be a skilled reader, a child does not have to partake of all four categories of reading purposes. But he/she must read to accomplish his/her own purposes, not just those of a teacher if he/she is to be truly considered a skilled reader.

Advanced Skilled Stage

In a real sense, the difference between humans and animals is our ability to symbolically represent thought and experience. Symbol systems have three characteristics; meaning, order, and surface representation. In print symbols, these elements are referred to as *semantics* (meaning), *syntax* or grammar (order etc.), and *visual array* and/or *grapho-phonics*. There are many symbolic print systems; music, mathematics, and "story" are some diverse examples. Maps, electrical diagrams, building blueprints, and graphs are examples of other symbolic print systems. Within "story" there are many genres, each of which may vary slightly in semantics, syntax, or graphic display. Chaucer, Shakespeare, and Tolstoi wrote in different genres. Fairy tales, tall tales, and legends are different genres that have similarities in semantics, syntax, and visual array. Blank verse, legal documents, and friendly letters are genres that have larger differences in semantics, syntax, and visual array. Golf scorecards, airline tickets, and catalogues have even greater differences. French, Chinese, and Arabic have obvious differences in visual array but also differ greatly in syntax and semantics. Math, music, and builders' blueprints have wide differences in the structure of their print systems.

A reader who is able to use the syntax, semantics, and visual array of a print system to construct meaning (i.e., to read) may remain functionally illiterate if he/she is severely limited in the number of genres or print systems he/she can successfully utilize in meeting his/her life needs. The wider the variety of print systems a reader can utilize for the construction of meaning, the greater his/her ability will be to meet his/her life needs.

To be functionally literate in our society, it is not enough to be able to utilize a narrow range of literacy genres. Skill in reading fairy tales, tall tales, and legends will not in itself allow a person to use reading to help solve daily life problems. Skill in utilizing a large variety of genres and print systems such as maps, catalogues, TV guides, tax forms, job applications, comics, racing guides, blue prints, etc. is necessary to produce a truly literate person.

To a large extent, as the child gets older, we need to help him/her learn to utilize an ever-expanding set of genres and print systems. The Reading Development Continuum at the advanced skilled stage attempts to measure the utilization the student makes of various print systems and genres.

N.B. Some people will become intensely skilled in all the nuances of a specific genre and may find using that genre an important part of their life's work there (i.e., an accountant, a tax lawyer, or a pharmacist). The ability to interpret and make meaning of a specific genre better than the average person attains a value that others pay to utilize.

When Reading Becomes Difficult

Normally children, will move through each of these stages as their reading develops. However, sometimes a child learns how *not* to read efficiently by concentrating too much on one reading cuing system and not enough on the other cuing systems, thus disrupting his/her use of the reading process.

Grapho-Phonic Fixated

Very often a child will have been led to overconcentrate on the grapho-phonic cuing system. The child will fixate on letters, trying to sound out each part of the word, or perhaps fixate on words, reading each word in a distinct, monotonic, jerky fashion. The skilled reader reads in groups of words, each group representing a meaningful unit. For example: The little boy — went to the store — and bought some gum.

Children can become fixated on word-by-word reading at the take-off stage, when you will sometimes notice the child "picking" each word off the page one by one as they read. Children can become fixated on letters by intense phonics programs or remedial reading programs that unindate the child with phonics until he/she forgets that the purpose of reading is to create meaning. Sometimes students in the take-off stage develop a grapho-phonic fixation simply because they become fascinated with the print.

Children before grade three are probably not yet fixated on grapho-phonics, but by grade three some children may well be. These children must be encouraged to use their knowledge of syntax and semantics to make predictions as to what will happen next in the story. They need guidance in using the grapho-phonic or visual array system to stimulate thought and to confirm or disconfirm their predictions.

Grapho-Phonic Transparent

Some children ignore the print. This condition is less common but more difficult to help a child overcome than overfixation on the print. The children learn as "self-conceptors" to "tell" a story that "makes story sense" and sounds like "story language" but does not conform to the actual print. These children make limited use of the visual array cuing system. Some well-intentioned "whole language teachers" encourage children to "guess" and do not give feedback when the "guess" is wrong because they do not wish to inhibit a child's willingness to "risk" an answer. Lack of constructive feedback to a child when his/her predictions are leading him/her away from constructing a meaningful text when reading is a serious impediment to the child's progress. A child must be helped to see both what reading is and what it isn't. The grapho-phonic transparent child has to be helped to attend to the print and to see the role of the grapho-phonic system in the reading process. Students need to learn the function of print in the reading process; that is, that the role of print is to stimulate thought and to confirm prediction.

ESL Readers

Children who speak English as a second language (ESL) may lack the information necessary for them to read in English. It is important for the teacher to distinguish between the ESL student who is already reading in his/her own language, and the ESL student who cannot read in any language. The reading process is similar in any language. As the ESL reader learns the English language, he/she will naturally apply his/her reading skills to this new language, provided his/her learning environment is rich in literacy demonstrations and he/she needs to read and write frequently to satisfy his/her own purposes.

The ESL non-reader must either be taught to read in his/her

own language of instruction if materials are available, or he/she must learn all aspects of the English language (listening, speaking, reading and writing) simultaneously. In either case, the process will take considerably longer than in the case of the ESL student who is already reading in his/her first language.

Disinterested Reader

At times children will be able to read, but are completely disinterested in reading. They do not see reading as furthering their own life purposes. They see reading as something they must do to further the teacher's purposes or needs. Their reading progress is hindered by their lack of a "need" to read. These children who are disinterested are an interesting challenge for whole language teachers.

Reading Development Continuum Placement Procedure

**Using Page 1 of the Reading Development Continuum
(See blackline masters)**

For young children in nursery, kindergarten, grade one or grade two, the teacher will need to record only on the first placement form. The teacher will need a pencil, paper, and several books of predictable material. If possible, children should bring some familiar print with which they have found success. Five minutes is all the time it should take to determine where the child is operating on the continuum.

Magical Stage

All children will be at least at the magical stage, learning the purpose of books. Through observation, we see the child playing with a book as with any other toy.

Self-Concepting Stage

Ask the child to read the familiar material he/she has with him/her. If the child "reads" the material and it sounds like a story but does not conform to the actual print, the child is at the self-concepting stage. Often a beginning self-conceptor at level one or two when asked "Where does it say that?" will point to a picture rather than the print. The later self-conceptor, levels three or four will point to the print on the page in response to that question. If the child does not have familiar print with him/her, give the child a storybook familiar to him/her, such as *The Three Little Pigs* or *Goldilocks and the Three Bears*, and ask the child to read it to you.

Bridging Stage

If the child reads a familiar story that roughly corresponds to the print, questions should be asked to see if he/she has memorized the story or is actually beginning to be stimulated by print. Such directions as "Please pick out the word(s) that says 'bears' or 'Goldilocks' or 'the end'" or ask questions like "What letter does that word start with?" or "What letter does the word end with?" If the child can answer these questions correctly he/she realizes the importance and role of print in reading. He/she is at the bridging stage.

If the child cannot find the words you ask him/her to, you should demonstrate by pointing to each word as you read. "Once upon a time there were three bears. Here is the word *time*. What does it start with?" Now ask the child to find *bears*. If he/she can now find *bears*, after your demonstration, he/she is an early bridger, just learning the role of print in reading.

Children who have been involved in a program rich in opportunities to write will also be able to write you a message and read it to you. They will be able to identify individual words in the message. These messages may be rich in "functional" spellings.

Take-Off Stage

When children reach the take-off stage, they show evidence that they are learning the process of reading, predicting, confirming or disconfirming, and incorporating this process into an ongoing construction of a story. Children are able to read familiar print in a variety of contexts. For example, the child may be able to read familiar print that says "Hickory, dickory, dock, the mouse ran up the clock." The teacher now writes, "I see a mouse on the clock." If the child reads these words, he/she is now in the take-off stage.

Independent Stage

If children have successfully completed the above task, the next step is to give them a simple predictable book that they have not encountered before. If they can read the book independently, they are independent readers.

Using Page 2 of the Reading Development Continuum
(See blackline masters)
Skilled and Advanced Skilled Stage

This is for older children, in grades 4 and above. By our definition, a skilled reader reads to further his/her life needs or purposes to read and write. The teacher will talk to students one-on-one at the beginning of a school year. The teacher will have with him/her many different genres of print; for example, a newspaper, a telephone book, a catalogue, an encyclopedia, an atlas, a menu, a bus schedule, a magazine, a science textbook, a poetry book, a comic book, a sports record book, The Guinness Book of Records, a T.V. guide, etc.

The teacher then asks a series of questions to see if a child can read to accomplish a purpose and to see if he/she has mastered the various print genres the teacher has available.

Sample Questions for Skilled and Advanced Skilled Stage

Questions such as the ones below focus on the child's ability to read for specific information.
1. Can you find out what would be on T.V. at 2 P.M. on Mondays?
2. Can you find Paris, France, on a map for me?
3. Can you find a way of ordering a pizza for me?
4. Can you find out how much a wheelbarrow might cost?

The following questions focus on whether the student reads to enjoy the experience of reading.
5. Have you read this summer for thirty minutes or more at one time.
6. What was the favorite book you read this summer?
7. Do you read a part of the paper each day?
8. What topics do you like to often read about?
9. Do you read any magazines?

Using Page 3 of the Reading Development Continuum

Page three of the Reading Development Continuum is used to record names of children who are having specific reading difficulties.

a) *Grapho-Phonic Transparent Readers.* These children are very easy to identify because even though they will "read" or tell a familiar story when confronted by print, they cannot find or point out specific words when asked to do so.

b) *Grapho-Phonic Fixated Readers.* These children are also easy to identify. They will sound out word parts if they have a "letter" fixation, or they will read each word distinctly and separately if they have a "word" fixation. In both cases they read in a monotone, and, when asked to tell you what the passage is about, their retelling of pertinent information is very limited. They do not know what the story is all about.

c) *Disinterested readers.* These children can read fluently and can retell details of the story. These children are identified by observing their reading habits over time. Their bulk reading records will identify them quickly. Children who are grapho-phonic transparent or graph-phonic fixated readers will also become disinterested in reading because they find reading to be nonsensical. The truly disinterested reader can make sense of reading but sees no purpose in doing so.

d) *ESL reader and ESL non-reader.* It will usually take a translator to determine how well a child reads in his/her own language. An interpreter talking with the child's parents can quickly determine if the child has learned to read in his/her native tongue.

Vygotsky's Zone of Proximal Development

Vygotsky's ideas have been a cornerstone of whole language, and whole language evaluation.

Vygotsky proposed that to understand children's learning, we must evaluate not only what they already know, but also we must find out what they are in the process of learning. Vygotsky proposed doing this by looking at tasks that children could perform with adult help but could not perform on their own. Vygotsky felt that the things a child could do only with adult help today are the things he/she would soon learn to do independently. If two children are both able to function independently at a typical seven year age level, but with adult help one can do things that a typical nine year old could do while the other can only do with adult help what a seven year six month child will do, then these two children are learning at different stages, despite both functioning at the same age level on the independent task. The tasks the child can do only with adult help are referred to as his/her zone of proximal development.

It is vital to find a child's zone of proximal development and to facilitate the child's learning at that level. Having the child repeat what he/she can already do is not engaging him/her in the most effective and productive learning activity. Presenting learning activities that the child cannot accomplish even with adult help is frustrating to the child. Learning activities in the zone of proximal development allow the child to build on and expand his/her knowledge. The conclusions we gain from Vygotsky's work are:

    a) It does matter what we teach, and the teacher does make a difference.

    b) We need to group children according to their needs, based on their similar zones of proximal development.

c) Membership in "needs groups" will continually change as children's zones of proximal development change.

d) Permanent ability groupings of any kind are by their nature always damaging to children's belief in themselves as capable learners. Permanent ability grouping fails to take into account that learning occurs in jumps as we suddenly fit ideas together into logical patterns.

Strategies for Use with Children in Different Stages of the Reading Development Continuum

For much of the day, children will work very well in completely heterogeneous activities. Children will absorb information from an activity that is sensible to them at the time. For example, if a class is modelling a poem, some children will stay very close to the model and write two or three verses. Other children will vary from the structure of the model in a creative way and may write dozens of verses. Each may have been successful in accomplishing the task in a way appropriate to his/her own stage of learning.

At times during the day, children will need specific activities that will draw their attention to the part of the reading process they are currently mastering. This grouping according to student needs, or needs grouping should occur for a part of each day's activities.

Magical Stage: A child who enters school never having been read to and coming from a home where there are no books may be at the magical stage in reading development. This child must learn the purpose of books and "book-handling skills."

Strategies

1. *Lap technique* - one-on-one reading with the child, using a picture book in a warm quiet setting.
2. *Shared books* - a big book shared by a teacher with a small group of children.
3. *Book Ownership* - the child is given his/her own storybook.

Self-Concepting Stage: The child is learning a sense of story, and the nonvisual cuing systems of syntax and semantics.

Strategies

1. *Reading* - read to the child several versions of the same story.
2. *Label books* - the child makes a scrapbook of product labels. Later, these labels, can be removed from their context by photo-copying to remove color and subsequently these labels can be written for the child to read.
3. *Oral Cloze* - the reader leaves out significant words when reading to a child so that the child can fill in the appropriate word.

Bridging Stage: The child becomes aware of the purpose of print.

Strategies

1. *I Can Read Folder* - the teacher and child collect familiar print that the child has found success with. The child has this material at his/her desk so that he/she can read and reread it, finding continued success with print. The "I Can Read" folder can be made up of poems, chants, daily classroom messages, a familiar book, or something the child has written.
2. *Minimal Cue Message* - the teacher and class build a message on the board about the day's activities.
3. *Rebuilding Familiar Print* - the teacher cuts familiar poems or small stories into chunks of meaning and mixes them up. The children put the print back together to match a correct copy.

Take-Off Stage: The child learns to use the reading process (predicting, confirming and integrating) to construct a meaning for the print.

Strategies

1. *Listening to the child read* - the child needs to read to a skilled reader every day.
2. *Supportive Readings (chants, choral readings and dramatic readings.)* - the take-off reader has a tendency to overconcen-

trate on the print and to read in a word-by-word manner. Chants, choral readings and dramatic readings, encourage the child to read for meaning and to chunk words into meaningful units.

3. *Comprehension Model* (see Reading, Writing and Caring, Cochrane et al 1984, for a full description). Although this strategy is important for all groups of children, it will help keep the take-off child's focus on reading as a thinking activity. It encourages readers to read from the point of view of a writer and sharpens the powers of prediction by helping students understand the power that using their prior knowledge has, in aiding comprehension. In this strategy students are taught to predict using their prior knowledge then verify their predictions with the print in an ongoing cyclical process.

Independent Stage — The child can read independently many complete books or other textual materials.
Strategies
1. Volume and Bulk Reading (See page 47). These activities help the child to practise the newly developed reading skills.
2. Research (See Reading, Writing and Caring for a full description). This helps the child broaden the purposes of reading to gain information about the world through their inquiry into content material.
3. Writing and reading different editions of the same story; e.g. six different versions of ''Jack and the Beanstalk.''
4. Point of view stories - the child reads a familiar story from the point of view of one of the other characters; e.g. *The True Story of the Three Little Pigs* by Jon Scieszka.

Grapho-Phonic Fixated: The child overattends to letters, sounds and words with the result that construction of meaning suffers.

Strategies

1. *Read-Along* - skilled reader and child read the same story aloud together. The skilled reader reads with expression and in chunks of meaning. The child is drawn along and cannot overconcentrate on the print.

2. *Written and Oral Retellings of Readings* - The child's focus is on creating and retaining the meaning of the print. Meaning becomes central.

3. *Chants, Choral Readings and Dramatic Readings* - because these readings are practiced group readings, the individual child is propelled through the readings by the group.

Grapho-Phonic Transparent: The child does not attends to print yet and "tells a story." In extreme cases, the child may say, "I can read this story with my eyes closed."

NB. Read-Along — This strategy does not work for the grapho-phonic transparent child. It is fine for the grapho-phonic fixated child, but the grapho-phonic transparent child will just echo the reader a split second later. This activity will not draw his/her attention to the print. This is a perfect example of how all strategies are not always appropriate for every stage of reading development.

Strategies

1. *"I can read" folder.* - This folder contains material at hand that the child is familiar with reading.

2. *Rebuilding familiar stories.*

3. *Writing a story for a wordless picture book.*

4. *Minimal Cue messages.*

This strategy encourages children to use prediction as a reading strategy by leaving out letters or words from a message, written on the blackboard by the teacher; i.e. d__w__n, w__th, v__w__ls. Children are lead to see that they can read without concentrating on every visual explanation of *minimal cues* please see Reading Writing and Caring.

Disinterested Stage: The child must come to see that reading can meet *his/her* life needs.

Strategies

1. *Double Agenda Activities* - The teacher's agenda is the reading and writing that will occur. The child's agenda is to get something done; e.g. the activity of having a class dance, or setting up a restaurant, or forming a club. The children value the activity but must read and write to make the activity happen.

2. *Teacher Demonstration* - The child sees a "significant other," the teacher, reading and discussing books and sharing his/her own writing.

3. *Interest Research* - Children carry out research and prepare material for sharing on topics of particular interest and importance to themselves.

Skilled Reader and Advanced Skilled Reader

The curriculum must be expanded to be meaningful to the needs and interests of children at this stage. They need to be exposed to an ever-widening variety of experiences and information and need time to sample knowledge and activities without having to master them in detail before going on. This was the original purpose of the junior high school and should be the focus of middle schools. Such a simple task as being able to us the phone book is often beyond many students, who may have not been shown how to use it properly. The curriculum should be based on the child and his/her interests and needs if the child is to become a highly skilled reader.

Grouping Children for Learning

Grouping children for learning is a very fluid process. The classroom can slip quickly from the whole class listening to a teacher's instructions to individuals writing their own ideas, and then to small groups of children sharing their ideas with each other.

In some situations, it is more effective and efficient for the teacher to treat the whole class as a single large group. Giving instructions at the introduction of a theme, whole class chanting of a poem, or a group unlocking of a big book may be most effective and efficient when done by a whole class.

In some situations, the whole class (or some of the students in the class) might work most effectively and efficiently as individuals. Practicing a skill, bulk reading, and an individual reading diagnosis are examples of individual activities.

There are two circumstances in which having small groups of children working together are the most effective and efficient way of grouping the class. First, children need to work in small groups of two to twelve students when language is being used to help solve a problem. There are many ways of forming these social groupings, be they random, student choice, or by common interest. The comprehension model, sharing in ''reader's workshop,'' and paired texts are activities used in these small group settings. Small groups are also used when the teacher is helping students with specific learning needs.

The learning activities selected to meet the students' needs could often best be done in one-to-one teaching/learning situations. However, one-to-one is often not efficient, as the teacher may not have the time to get around to all the students individually. It may also not be effective in all cases to work with the child in a one-on-one situation, because working in a larger social unit often provides a better learning situation for the child. The Reading Development Continuum helps identify children who are at a common stage of learning and who therefore have common learning needs that will respond to common teaching strategies. That is the basis for needs groupings.

R.D.C. PAGE 1   N.B. Use different color ink for each date's observation

Grade __one__
Teacher __O. Cochrane__
Date __September__ (horizontal-line shading)
Date __December__ (crosshatch shading)
Date __April__ (×× mark)
Date _____

NAME	M1	M2	SC1	SC2	SC3	SC4	B1	B2	B3	B4	TO1	TO2	TN1	TN2	TN3	TN4
MAGICAL (M1–M2)			**SELF-CONCEPTOR** (SC1–SC4)				**BRIDGING** (B1–B4)				**TAKE-OFF** (TO1–TO2)		**INDEPENDENT** (TN1–TN4)			
Jane Block							××	××	××							
John Doe														××	××	
Paul Frank									××							
Andy Gill				××												
Mary Hill															××	××
Sally Jones						××	××									
David Jones																××
Harry Mills									××	××	××	××				
Pat Moll																
Janet Molly														××		
Ralph Peterson														××	××	××
Dorothy Potter								××	××							
Fred Slatz							××	××	××							
Jeff Solsky									××							
Bill Tall														Moved Jan. 29th		
Jean Tappy							××	××								
Ron Tell													××			
Mary Teplepski					××	××										
Betty Upe							××									
Marie Zalk															××	
Jane Doll		Transfer in March 19th					××									

Forming Temporary Specific Needs Groupings

September Needs Groupings

Self-Conceptors	Bridgers	Take-Off & Independent
Jane Black	John Doe	Mary Hill*
Andy Gill	Paul Frank	David Jones
Sally Jones	Dorothy Potter*	Pat Moll
Harry Mills	Jean Zappy	Janet Molly*
Fred Slatz	Ron Tell*	Ralph Peterson
Jeff Solsky		Bill Tall
Mary Teplipski		Marie Zalk
Betty Upe		

*These children were right on the borderline between stages. The teacher makes decisions as to which needs group they would grow best in and is prepared to move these children to another group if they do not respond well to the material and strategies used with the group in which they have been placed.

December Needs Groupings

Self-Conceptors	Bridgers	Take-Off	Independent
Andy Gill	Jane Black*	Bill Tall	John Doe
Fred Slatz*	Paul Frank	Ron Tell	Mary Hill
Mary Teplipski	Sally Jones*		David Jones
	Harry Mills		Pat Moll —▶
	Dorothy Potter		Janet Molly
	Jeff Solsky		Ralph Peterson
	Jean Zappy		Marie Zalk
	Betty Upe		

—▶ Needs challenge. Find individual project to work on.

April Needs Groupings

Self-Conceptors	Bridgers	Take-Off	Independent
Andy Gill	Jane Black	Harry Mills	John Doe
	Paul Frank*	Dorothy Potter*	Mary Hill
	Sally Jones	Jean Zappy	David Jones
	Fred Slatz	Ron Tell	Pat Moll —▶
	Jeff Solsky*	Betty Upe	Janet Molly
	Mary Teplipski		Ralph Peterson —▶
	Jane Doll		Marie Zalk

Important Reminders

1. For most activities, such as "writers workshop" and volume reading, children will not be in needs groups.

2. Needs groups are fluid and change each time children are placed on the Reading Development Continuum. Based on daily observations of a child, the teacher will often move the child to another group between RDC testings.

3. For a period of time each day, children will be engaged in specific learning activities designed to meet their needs. These activities will help them to advance in their understanding of what reading is.

    Self-conceptors need to have their attention drawn to the non-visual cuing systems.

    Take-off students need to read aloud to a proficient reader each day.

    Independent students need lots of time to practice reading.

4. Some students marked by the symbol —▶ are ready to enter the skilled reading stage and need to participate in projects that allow reading to further their life purposes.

Sample II of Grouping Children for Learning

R.D.C. PAGE 2

N.B. Use different color ink for each date's observation

Grade __six__
Teacher __Mr. Leggero__
Date __September__
Date _____
Date _____
Date _____

NAME	SKILLED				ADVANCE SKILLED										Other Genres	
	INFORMATION	ENTERTAINMENT	READ TO READ	MAINTENANCE OF SELF	NARRATIVE	POETRY	TV GUIDES	GRAPHS	MAPS	ENCYCLOPEDIA RESEARCH	HISTORICAL	MAGAZINES	CATALOGUES	TELEPHONE BOOKS		
Hank Ball	✔	✔	✔		✔	✔	✔	✔	✔	✔	✔	✔	✔	✔		
Melody Carp		✔	✔		✔	✔						✔	✔			
Jim Farmer	✔	✔	✔		✔	✔	✔	✔	✔			✔				
Harold Gill	✔	✔	✔	✔	✔	✔	✔	✔	✔	✔	✔	✔	✔			
Bill Lude	✔	✔	✔	✔	✔	✔	✔	✔	✔	✔	✔	✔	✔	✔		
Mary Molly	✔	✔			✔	✔	✔			✔		✔	✔	✔		
Barb Murphy	✔	✔	✔	✔	✔	✔	✔					✔	✔	✔		
Colin Nice	✔	✔			✔	✔		✔	✔	✔	✔					
Sam Maine	✔	✔	✔		✔	✔	✔	✔		✔	✔		✔			
Sidney Ort	✔	✔	✔		✔	✔	✔	✔	✔	✔	✔	✔		✔		
Jane Ozinski	✔			✔	✔	✔						✔	✔			
Mark Short	✔	✔			✔	✔					✔			✔		
Todd Treely	✔	✔			✔	✔	✔	✔			✔	✔	✔			
Anne Wong	✔			✔	✔		✔	✔	✔	✔		✔	✔			

Discussion of Sample II

In September, the teacher has tried to see which of his students read for real-life purposes (are skilled readers). The teacher also begins to see how many different genres the students can process successfully. During the year, the teacher will try to help those members of the class who cannot functionally read TV guides, maps, graphs, catalogues, etc. The teacher will also introduce additional genres as the year progresses and will test their use.

Sample III of Grouping Children for Learning

R.D.C. PAGE 3

N.B. Use different color ink for each date's observation

Grade six
Teacher B. Flett
Date September
Date _____
Date _____
Date _____

Level 1 indicates highest degree of difficulty for the child.

NAME	Grapho-Phonic Transparent				Grapho-Phonic Fixated				Disinterested				ESL Reader		ESL Non Reader	
	1	2	3	4	1	2	3	4	1	2	3	4	1	2	1	2
Jane Block									▓							
John Doe					▓											
Paul Frank					▓	▓										
Andy Gull									▓							
Mary Hill					▓											
Sally Jones									▓							
David Jones	▓															
Harry Mills									▓							
Pat Moll									▓							
Janet Molly										▓						
Ralph Peterson					▓											
Dorothy Potter									▓							

In the preceding example, a teacher has taken over a grade six class in September and finds that many children are avoiding reading. By looking at these children with the Reading Development Continuum, the teacher finds that there are three different reasons for the problem. Each of the reasons identified for the reluctance to read needs to be approached in a different manner.

In each of the categories, there are levels. Level 1 indicates the highest degree of difficulty in each category and level 4 the lowest degree of difficulty.

Discussion of Sample III

David Jones is found to be grapho-phonic transparent, that is, he pays too little attention to the Grapho-Phonic cuing system (visual array). David has been heard to remark ''I can read this story with my eyes shut'' as he reads a familiar book to the teacher. The teacher must structure situations that will draw David's attention to the print and its role in the reading process.

John Doe, Paul Frank, Mary Hill, and Ralph Peterson over-concentrate on the grapho-phonic cuing system. John and Mary read letters (flamingo as fla-m-ing-o). Paul and Ralph read one word at a time with little comprehension of the complete passage. These children need to be encouraged to read for meaning, with expression, and in chunks of meaning for a specific purpose. Read-Along, chants and dramatic readings are some useful activities for them.

Jane Block, Andy Gull, Sally Jones, Harry Mills, Pat Moll, Janet Molly, and Dorothy Potter can all read but choose not to. They are disinterested in reading and only do so when the teacher forces them. They might benefit from double agenda work, research projects, and an interest inventory to make sure the classroom contains materials of specific interest to these students.

The Reading Card

The reading card is a simple but functional record-keeping tool. In whole language classrooms, a student's unrehearsed oral reading is seen as a way of looking into a child's mind. It is through the child's miscues in his/her reading that insights into the child's reading process is revealed. The child's miscues tell us how the cuing systems are being used in the reading process and the child's strategies for predicting, confirming or disconfirming, and integrating into the overall meaning.

Teachers in whole language classrooms listen to each child read on a regular basis. The teacher should have a reading card for each child (a large recipe card works well), and it is on this card that the teacher records observations of the child's reading of challenge level materials. How often these observations are recorded will depend on what stage the child is at and the amount of time the teacher puts aside for this. It is very important though, that at least one recording should be made every two to three weeks for primary children and every three to four weeks for students above grade three. After individual observations have been made, students can be grouped according to need in order to teach appropriate strategies. After a series of lessons have been taught, another observation should be made in order to assess the effectiveness of the strategies that have been taught.

All observations should be *dated*. The following is a list of ideas or questions the teacher may want to keep in mind when listening to a child read.
1. Does the child ask him/herself the following questions:
   — Does what I read make sense?
   — Does what I read sound like language?
2. Does the child read with chunks of meaning? (That is, does the

child use good phrasing as opposed to word-by-word reading?)

3. What strategies does the child use when he/she comes to a word he/she doesn't know? Does the reader know which are the preferred strategies of good readers, such as:

   a) Guessing - that is, prediction based on reader's prior knowledge.
   b) Skipping - reading ahead for more information in order to figure out the word.
   c) Rereading for more information.
   d) Taking the time to *stop* and think what the word could be, based on the context and content of the story.
   e) Giving word or place holders for difficult proper names.
   f) Skipping the word altogether.

Does the reader use the following less-preferred strategies? They are less preferred because it takes the reader's focus away from meaning.

   a) Sounding out the difficult word.
   b) Starting his/her mouth with the sound of the first letter in the hope that the rest of the word will follow.
   c) Looking for word parts such as *ing* in "work*ing*" or *for* in "in*for*mation" or *apple* and *cart* in "*applecart.*"

Does the reader use the following strategies that take the reader away from independence?

   a) Asking someone else what the word is.
   b) Looking up the word in a dictionary.

4. Does the child read quickly enough to make meaning?

5. Does the child predict what will happen next on the basis of what he/she already knows, such as:

   a) how stories fit together, that is his/her knowledge of story grammar and story patterns.
   b) how associative and imbedded schema work.
   c) how stories relate to other stories.

6. Does the child have awareness of the Reading and Writing contract? Consider such questions as these:
    a) Is the child picking up the clues that the writer is giving?
    b) Does the child know that the author's job is to give the reader enough information to make sense of the piece and that it is a reader's job to pick up the clues?
7. Is the child able to do a good retelling of what has just been read?

When the teacher records the observations, only some of these need to be recorded at any one time. The following might be some of the observations of a grade two student's reading in September.

Sample Reading Card

John Doe — Grade 2
Sept. 5/91 — Read *Franklin in the Dark* by Paulette Bourgeois

Reading was held up because of character names he doesn't know. John tends to use the sounding-out strategy exclusively when he comes to an unknown word. He likes his reading to be expressive, so he is frustrated by unknown words.
— Some strategy lessons needed on place holders for names
— Do some lessons on skipping unknown words

Sept. 17/91 — Read *Roll Over!* by Mordicai Gerstein

Good use of prediction strategy on the sentence pertaining to what family member fell out and what animal still might be in the bed. John predicted Sister Squirrel fell out but on actual reading he read Sister Seal. His first strategy is still to sound out unknown words. More lessons on predicting and skipping strategies for unknown words are needed. John enjoyed this book.

Sept. 30/91 — Read *Bear's Toothache* by David McPhail

When John came to unknown words, he still wanted to try sounding it out first but would look at me and say, ''Oh yes, I should just skip it.'' John is a confident reader and is trying to use new strategies for unknown words.

Bulk Reading

We learn to read by reading. The more we read, the more effective and efficient readers we become. In whole language classrooms, students are encouraged to read to themselves, to read as part of a group during novel studies, to read at home, and to read to their friends and to their parents.

A good reading program will provide students with time to read. To be able to read for sixty minutes at a time is a good skill to have. A good reading program also provides students with a variety and choice of books. Dan Fader said there should be 1000 books in each classroom, and that newspapers, magazines, menus, and sports information, such as baseball cards, should be included in the classroom reading display. A good reading program will also ensure that children use the stories they have read by sharing or retelling them or by using them as launch pads to creative expression during writing or storytelling.

It is vital that whole language teachers see that records are kept of their students' reading. The books a child has read as well as the total number of pages he/she has read is valuable information to share with parents.

At a parent interview meeting in February, we might share the following with parents:

"John has read 2650 pages from 46 books this year. The average number of pages read by each student in the class is 1890. He reads a wide variety of materials and enjoys sharing these books with others. John is having no difficulty in reading."

"Sally has read 17 books with 337 pages. The average number of pages read by each student in the class is 1890. She is most comfortable with books with few pages in them. She does not like to share the books she has read, but will read aloud willingly to others when asked to. I can't seem to find material that really excites Sally. Maybe you can help by sharing with me the things Sally really likes to do. Then I will try to find some books about those activities. Maybe you can listen to her read at home in the evening and I will listen to her at school. Her reading growth will depend upon us helping her to read more.''

''Jason has read 8792 pages from 41 books. The average number of pages read by each student in the class is 1890. He has read *The Hobbit* and *The Lord of the Rings* series. I have to borrow books from the grade six classroom library to keep up with his reading appetite. He is not very keen on sharing ideas he finds in these books; he just likes to read as much as he can.''

Although Sally (above) has already read as many pages this year as would be found in a typical basal reader, it is clear that she is not an enthusiastic, effective and efficient reader. Clearly the information from the bulk reading records indicates we must make a specific plan to help Sally grow as a reader.

John is reading a wide variety of books that shows he is a very successful reader in a grade four program.

Jason is precocious in his reading habits. The number and complexity of the books he chooses show a reader who should be extremely successful in literacy activities. The goal now for Jason would be to make the reading and writing connection and help his precocious reading find expression in his writing.

Children will read in many situations. All books they read can be included in their bulk reading record. This may include books read at home and books read as part of a group in novel studies. As teachers become more involved in strong writing programs, the amount of reading students do sometime drops as less emphasis is placed upon the reading aspect of the language arts program. Writing is important but it should not limit a child's reading. 5000 pages of print in a year per student is a good average for a student in grade five or six. A child's reading is the foundation of his/her writing. The child should read like a writer while he/she is reading and let the reading influence the writing.

For a fuller discussion of ''Bulk Reading'' see *Reading, Writing and Caring*.

**BULK READING
RECORD SHEET**

	TITLE	AUTHOR	PAGES	DATE COMPLETED	FOLLOW UP
1.					
2.					
3.					
4.					
5.					
6.					
7.					
8.					
9.					
10.					
		TOTAL			

Student's Reflections: _____

_____

_____

Reading Plan: _____

_____

_____

Teacher's Comments: _____

_____

_____

EXAMPLE

BULK READING RECORD SHEET

GRADE _____ ROOM _____

NAME __John Smith__

SHEET NUMBER __4__

	TITLE	AUTHOR	PAGES	DATE COMPLETED	FOLLOW UP
1.	Skinnybones	Barbara Park	112	Jan. 10	Did a book sell to a friend
2.	Sounder	William Armstrong	116	Jan. 19	Drew a new book cover
3.	Soup	Robert Newton Peck	96	Jan. 23	Made a bookmark for Soup to stay in the book
4.	Soup and Me	Robert Newton Peck	115	Jan. 27	I drew a picture of soup
5.	Soup in the Saddle	Robert Newton Peck	110	Feb. 2	I didn't do a follow up this time
6.	Stone Fox	John Reynolds Gardiner	81	Feb. 4	I wrote a new chapter about Stone Fox
7.	Monsters He Mumbled	Sean O'Huigin	28	Feb. 6	I read a poem to my dad
8.	Amigo	Byrd Baylor	41	Feb. 6	I wrote a letter to Byrd Baylor
9.	The Hockey Sweater	Roch Carrier	22	Feb. 8	I brought my hockey card collection to school
10.	Prince Cinders	Babette Cole	29	Feb. 9	I rewrote the story, my way
		TOTAL	750		

Student's Reflections: __I read the two best books of my life; Stone Fox and Skinnybones.__
Stone Fox made me cry. I never cried over a book before. I split a gut laughing over Skinnybones.

Reading Plan: __I would like to find some "different" kinds of books. Maybe I'll read some__ more poetry.

Teacher's Comments: I cried over Stone Fox too. For poetry I recommend "New Kid on the Block" by Jack Prelutsky. For something "different" I really liked "On the Trail of the Fox" by Claudia Schnieper. The book has great pictures and factual information about foxes. Or, how about a joke book? You might enjoy "Tickle Yourself With Riddles" by Michael Smollin.

Reading — Status of the Class

Whole language teachers need to modify, adapt, and create evaluation strategies that will meet the evaluation needs of their classrooms. Susan Macfarlane is a grade 5 teacher at Shaughnessy Park School in Winnipeg, Canada, who has developed a strategy for analyzing her students' Bulk Reading cards and designing prescriptions to further her students interest and involvement in reading. Susan's reading plans for her students are designed to help groups of students who seem to have common needs for their further reading and to address individual student needs.

The value of the Bulk Reading student record card is greatly enhanced by the periodic, thoughtful analysis of the information on them. A "Reading - Status of the Class" Summary, two or three times a year is an excellent method to keep on top of the reading needs of the class and of the individual students.

A sample of one of Susan's "Reading - Status of the Class records" follows.

READING — STATUS OF THE CLASS
AND INDIVIDUALIZED GOALS

— teacher's reflection   *teacher's plan

Joan
- — Reads mostly Garfield, Snoopy Books, short primary books.
- * Try to interest her in shorter, more difficult (higher level) books. (Pee Wee Scouts)

Bob
- — Disliked reading in September - wasted time. New interest in Judy Delton books in Nov.
- — Eager to read, likes Pee Wee Scouts series
- * Keep the interest - more Pee Wee books, write reviews, help shop for new books for the class

Paul	—	Started with Garfield books, found an interest in *Jeffrey,* & Third Grade Ghost books
	*	Help find an interest - better record keeping, more Jeffrey books
John	—	Started with Garfield, Snoopy, primary books
	—	Interest is now in "Choose Your Own Adventure" books. Tries a lot of books but does not continue "uninteresting ones"
	*	Encouragement - choose other adventures in same book.
Mary	—	Continued to read a lot of short primary books, joke books, Snoopy, Garfield books, variety of genres
	*	Introduce her to some challenging material, nonfiction??
Mark	—	Reads very slowly, concentrates on longer (100 page) books. Reads a variety of material
	*	Encouragement - introduce shorter, higher interest books
Anne	—	Reads a variety of books, consistent in finishing
	*	Introduce different genres, nonfiction.
Harold	—	Reads a lot of short lower level books. Capable of reading more challenging material (reads newspaper)
	*	Encourage higher level - more challenging material
Sue	—	Wastes reading time - no interest
	—	Recording skills weak
Judy	—	Independent reader. Enjoys books about teenage girls. Reads a variety of genres
	*	Help choose some challenging books - Grade 6 room may have some for her.
Fay	—	Reads a variety of genres (fic/nonfic/jokes)
	—	Most books are lower level
	*	Help choose a higher level book ie. *James and the Giant Peach*

Beth	—	Beth reads a variety of genres (myths, fairytales, fiction) Could read higher level
	*	Encourage higher level - Roald Dahl's, *James & the Giant Peach*
Kurt	—	Lack of interest. Spends most time looking for books. Most are joke books.
	*	Find interest area, set reading routine - monitor
Tess	—	Reads consistently - spends a lot of time on book
	*	Should be exposed to higher level books Should be encouraged to keep reading, has started on own to read more difficult books
Al	—	Independent Reader - reads a variety of books (animals, adventure, mystery)
	*	Allow choice from another room. Look out for interest books from our class, make new material available.
Doug	—	Lower level books, disinterested reader
	*	Conference, find interests, suggest some books. Monitor daily.
Nathan	—	Reads a variety of books, shorter, lower level. Looses interest quickly - found Pee Wee books, just started 2nd book.
	*	Find high interest books, action to keep interest. Conference - make a reading plan.
Billy	—	Lower level (primary) books - a lot of Snoopy, and Garfield books.
	*	Conference - find interests, suggest material.
Ed	—	Started with lower level books, reads a lot of ''Choose Your Own Adventure''
	*	Encourage to read different adventures in one book (instead of reading 10-20 pages of a 100 page book) Discuss: choices, why certain adventures are better.
Jake	—	Nonreader at beginning - wasted time. Now has taken off - interested. Routine reading time.
	*	Continue to help find interesting books. Discuss books with him verbally, then move to written responses.

READING — STATUS OF THE CLASS
GROUP GOALS

Date: Feb 18/91

	Name	Completed Books	Pages
	Joan	24	1231
B	Bob	14	875
B	Paul	8	584
	John	31	2185
	Mary	55	2859
A	Mark (Nov-Feb)	5	483
	Anne	15	1191
	Harold	29	1598
A	Sue	16	959
	Judy	29	2809
	Fay	26	1187
	Beth	23	1505
A	Kurt	17	1099
A	Tess	9	427
	Al	14	1541
A	Doug	7	414
B	Nathan	16	682
	Billy	20	1116
B	Ed	52	1880
B	Jake (Nov 28-Feb)	7	353
	Valdine ▶	New Students Jan-Feb	
	Raylene ▶		

GOALS

FOR ALL STUDENTS

Goals - Novel study (2nd)
- partner reading   all students
- comprehension models

GROUP A

Concentrate on students who have not found a genuine interest in reading and who do not choose to read books.

Provide incentive to read with fun, enjoyable reading activities (comprehension models, paired reading) — Kurt, Mark, Doug, Sue, Tess

GROUP B

These students have started to take off. They show interest in a certain author or type of book and now choose to read books.

Provide books they are interested in to develop a love for reading. Provide every opportunity to discuss books they have read. — Bob, Jake, Nathan, Ed, Paul.

Story Retelling - with a Story Grammar Grid

Question:

How can you tell if a student understands what he/she has read?

Answer: Ask the student.

If the student can tell you what happened in the story, then obviously he/she has understood what has been read. By retelling stories, children demonstrate that they understand those stories. As well, the act of retelling helps the child consciously control the information of the text.

Using a grammar grid provides a framework for the retelling and makes the process of retelling and the recording of the child's retelling much quicker. This is crucial because classroom teachers cannot afford to use evaluation procedures that are inefficient, timewise.

This procedure also allows you to come up with a comprehension score out of 100. Do not be seduced by the seeming clarity of a number score. Like all number scores, the number itself has considerably less value than the process by which the number is obtained, that is, the observation of the child in action.

Procedure

1. Select a short, problem-centered story that is not familiar to the class.
2. After you have read the story, fill in the story grammar grid.
3. Reread the story to see if there is other important information to be placed on the grid.
4. Assign marks to the various segments of the grammar grid so that they total 100. In each story, differing segments of the

story grammar grid will assume more or less importance. For example, in some stories, understanding the setting will be essential to comprehension of the story. In some stories, how the characters feel (the internal reaction) may dominate the story. In others, the outcome or ending contains the essence of the story.

5. At this point, it is important for you to recognize that there is no one right answer when retelling a story. Our interpretation of the story must remain flexible as we look at and evaluate the child's retelling.

6. Have a student read the story aloud to you.

7. Ask the child to retell the story to you when he/she has finished reading it.

8. Check off on a copy of your story grid answer sheet all the information the child tells you about the story.

9. Now do an assisted retelling to gather more information about the story from the child. In doing the assisted retelling, you ask the child to elaborate on information already given.
   For example; ''You mentioned there was a genie in the story. Can you tell me more about the genie, like what he did, or what he looked like?'' You also search for other information the child may know but did not tell in the initial retelling. This is done by asking questions such as these; ''Was there any one else in the story? What happened after . . . ?''

10. Now total the score out of 100 that the child has attained.

11. A relatively high score indicates good comprehension of this story by the child. A relatively low score indicates relatively poor comprehension of this story by the child.

12. Finally, if the child shows poor comprehension of the story it is important for the teacher to discover the reason for the child's poor comprehension of the story. Some reasons for poor comprehension are:

a) The child may be using the reading process inefficiently. Often poor comprehension is the result of overattention to the grapho-phonic (visual array) cuing system.

b) The child may be unfamiliar with the genre or structure of the story.

c) The child may lack a background of experience with the semantic elements of the story.

d) The child may be reading too slowly, for effective comprehension to occur. If the child reads slower than a rate of about two hundred words per minute, comprehension is made more difficult. Word-by-word readers experience this kind of comprehension distortion.

e) The story may simply be poorly written, thus making it inherently difficult for persons of more limited literary experience to comprehend.

f) The children may not be motivated to want to comprehend the story. They may not see any purpose for themselves in this activity.

Sample Short Story for Use with the Story Grammar Grid

MODERN FAIRY TALES — SON AND GENIE
by Orin Cochrane

Not very long ago and not too far away, there lived a little boy who was very unhappy. He was unhappy because he couldn't catch flies. Albert Rand could catch flies. Albert could catch flies in his hand. He caught them as they sat on his desk or he caught them right out of the air as they flew by. Everyone in class liked Albert because he was the best fly catcher in the whole world.

And the boy was also sad because he couldn't tell stories. Every time he would try to tell a joke or a story, he would stutter and stammer or forget the punch line. Not that that mattered, because no one ever listened to him anyway. Eddy Winder could tell stories. Eddy told the funniest jokes and everyone laughed. Everyone liked Eddy because he was the best storyteller in the whole world.

His mom said not to worry. "You're smart," she said, "and that is more important than catching flies or telling stories."

Moms sure can be dumb sometimes because you sure don't have many friends just being smart, but if he could only catch flies . . . even one . . .

One day the sad little boy was playing in the attic and he found a strange blue bottle that his dad had brought home from the faraway city of Baghdad. His father said that he had bought it in a bazaar, whatever a bazaar is. As he was playing with the bottle, the boy pulled the cork out of its top. Suddenly there was a huge puff of smoke pouring out of the bottle and a Genie appeared.

"Oh Master," said the Genie, "your wish is my command. In fact" continued the Genie, "any of three wishes are my commands."

"Wow," said the little boy, "do you really mean it? I can really have three wishes?"

"Yes, you may," replied the Genie, "and then I will be free."

"Oh, how I wish that I could catch flies. I wish I were the best fly catcher in the world," the boy exclaimed.

Just then a fly flew by. The boy shot out his left hand and caught the fly between his finger and thumb. "Wow!" he said, "not even Albert Rand could do that" and he had done it with his left hand, too.

Back into the bottle went the Genie and off to school went the boy. Everyone was amazed at the skill he had at catching flies. His friends crowded around him and watched as he snared seventeen flies. He was about to break Albert's world record of nineteen when Eddy Winder came up and started to tell a new joke. And no one was watching when the little boy caught four flies at once and set a new world fly-catching record.

That night the boy went back up to the attic and once more pulled the cork from the bottle. In a cloud of smoke, the Genie appeared again.

"Your wish is my command, Master," said the Genie. "As a matter of fact, any two wishes are my commands.''

''I wish I could tell jokes and stories better than anyone else in the whole world,'' said the little boy. Immediately he thought of a funny story that he just had to tell his mom and dad. The Genie went back into the bottle. The boy went downstairs and told his story. His mom and dad both laughed so hard that tears rolled down their cheeks.

The next day the happy little boy went to school and caught flies and told the most hilarious stories anyone had ever heard. His friends crowded around him all day long to hear his stories and to watch him set the new world record for catching flies. Thirty-nine flies he caught, including seven with one grab. He hardly had time to go to the library to do his research assignment.

He decided to write a paper on genies and began reading a book about them. What he read made his blood run cold. It said in the book that after granting the third wish, a Genie was free and could not be commanded to return to his bottle. As well as that, Genies were evil and once freed could do great damage, sometimes even eating the person to whom they had just granted three wishes.

It was a good thing that the little boy was smart. He resolved to go home right away and use his third wish to make the Genie stay in that blue bottle forever. The boy ran home and just as he got near his house, his dog, Rex, ran out to meet him and was struck down by a car. Rex was badly hurt and the boy's father said that he must be brave for his dog would surely die.

Quick as a flash the boy ran up to the attic. He pulled the cork from that strange blue bottle and out popped the Genie.

''Oh, I wish that my dog, Rex, would be all right,'' the boy cried.

Immediately, through the window, he heard his father say, ''Look, Rex is getting up. He's running about. He is going to be all right.'' The little boy was so happy.

But the Genie laughed a most evil laugh and shouted, ''Now I'm free. For the second time in a thousand years, I'm free,'' he cried in glee. Then the Genie changed himself into a giant tiger and padded up to the little boy and said, ''I am all powerful and I can do anything and now I am going to eat you up.''

''Shucks,'' replied the little boy, ''you can eat me up if you want but I don't believe this all-powerful stuff. So you can change yourself into a tiger, big deal.'' And the boy plucked a long whisker out of the tiger's face.

The Genie was enraged. ''I am so all-powerful,'' he roared. ''Can't you see that I have just changed myself into a fierce and ferocious tiger?''

''Yes,'' replied the boy, with a bored yawn, ''I can see that, but can you do any difficult tricks?''

''Well, how about this trick!'' screamed the Genie. And with a puff of smoke he changed himself from a tiger into a fire-breathing dragon and walked toward the boy saying, ''And now I am really going to eat you up because I am the all-powerful Genie.''

''Well, sufferin' succotash,'' the boy said, ''o'course you can eat me up, but don't tell me this all-powerful nonsense." And he told the Genie a story about a magician so all-powerful that he could change himself into absolutely anything. He could change into a drop of water or a second of time or even into the hush of a silent night. The Genie listened, fascinated, as the boy told the most interesting story in the world. "That magician was the most 'all-powerful' being ever. He could change himself into absolutely anything except the most difficult feat of all. The magician could not change himself into a fly."

"Oh well," beamed the Genie, "I am the most powerful being after all." And in a puff of smoke the Genie became a fly buzzing around the room.

In a flash, the boy's hand shot out and grabbed that fly and threw him back into the blue bottle and stuffed the cork into the top.

"Well," sighed the boy, picking his teeth with the tiger whisker, "maybe Mom was right. Being smart is most important after all."

And so the little boy walked downstairs with his tiger whisker in his hand. "I think I'll go ask my dad how he got his tiger whisker," the boy said.

THE END

SAMPLE RETELLING OF SON AND GENIE USING A GRAMMAR GRID

		EPISODE #I	EPISODE #II	EPISODE #III
Setting 10 (3*+3*+4)	Who	boy* Mom Eddy Winder genie* Dad Albert Rand	dog	tiger
	When 2	not long ago		
	Where 2	not far away		
	What 4	boy is unhappy because he has no friends		fire-breathing dragon
Initiating Event or Problem 24 (3x8)		genie appears and offers the boy three wishes	boy's dog is hit by car and will surely die	genie wants to eat boy
Internal Reaction 6 (3x2)	Emotion	boy is excited	boy is sad	fear
	Plan 6 (3x2)	boy will wish to catch flies and be able to tell stories	use 3rd wish to save dog	trick the genie
External Reaction or Attempt 6 (3x2)		wishes to catch flies wishes to tell good stories	wishes that his dog would be O.K.	tells story to get genie to change to a fly. catches fly. put fly in bottle.
Outcome 30 (10x3)		boy has friends boy can catch flies boy can tell stories	dog is OK genie is free	fly (genie) is back in the bottle and can do no harm
Ending 10 (2x5)				boy happy dad's tiger whisker
TOTAL 100 TEACHER REFLECTIONS		TEACHER COMMENTS ON HOW CHILD RETOLD THE STORY AND ON ANY FACTORS THAT MAY HAVE AFFECTED THE CHILD'S RETELLING.		Score _____

Writing Evaluation

Writing evaluation is worthwhile only when it leads to more effective and joyous writing by children.

A Changing View of Writing

Our view of what writing is and how it should be evaluated has changed dramatically as a result of the last twenty-some years of research and observation. We no longer see writing as a pouring out of ideas or stories but as a construction of meaning. Because writing is seen as a means for constructing new meaning rather than a mere recording of preconceived ideas, major shifts have taken place in our total view of writing and writing evaluation. Shifts have taken place in the following areas.

1. *Student purposes as opposed to teacher purposes for writing.* In the past, students were given writing assignments by the teacher. For the most part, students didn't have a real purpose of their own for writing the piece, other than to satisfy teacher needs. We now understand that when writers have a purpose for writing that is relevant to their needs, better pieces of writing are produced. Purpose drives the piece, purpose determines the process the writer will go through to produce the piece. The purpose of the piece will determine also the nature of the product that is produced by the writer; that is, the best form in which to couch that particular meaning. Thus, it is purpose that determines whether the final product will be a poem, a letter, an essay, or an advertisement. So in fairness to our students, pieces of writing that are to be evaluated should be those in which the purpose of the piece is relevant to the writer's needs.

2. *Process and product are both critical aspects in the writing evaluation.* We have all seen many swings in education. At one time, only product in writing was considered for evaluation. Then we saw the pendulum swing to process. We saw lots of writing going on in classrooms but not many finished pieces

were produced, and those that were completed, were often only of personal interest to the writer and his/her friends. We simply jumped from one boat to another instead of seeing both process and product as areas of focus in evaluation. Just evaluating a finished piece cannot give enough information to be helpful to writers for their next piece. Just evaluating the process also has limited strength for the writer in the construction of the next piece. It is when both aspects are considered in evaluation that writers can get information that will help them grow in their craft of writing.

3. *Meaning and form are no longer separated.* Form helps us to express meaning better. At one time, we had so much emphasis on form that students all over the country were given numerous assignments pertaining to grammar and punctuation and very little work was done with the actual construction of meaning. For the most part, students were given the impression that it didn't matter so much *what* you said as *how* you said it. Meaning and form are both important in effective writing and must not be seen as separate entities. As we respond to a student's writing, we must respond so that our students see meaning and form as integrated concepts. Form shapes meaning and meaning alters form.

4. *Building on the strengths of the writer is a more effective way of developing skills than by error hunting.* There was a time when evaluation of writing was done with a red pen that sought to mark errors in the writing. It was believed that by having students fix these errors, they would become better writers. Indeed, that piece of writing may have improved by correcting the errors, but it did not improve the writer's strategies for the next piece. In fact, this kind of evaluating serves to turn many students away from writing. The process of learning to write is now seen to be like any other kind of learning; that is, the writer needs to know his/her own strengths and seek to extend these strengths.

All of us respond to success in what we are trying to do and find it to be motivating. Evaluation of writing should leave the writer wanting to write again. The evaluation should be motivating to the writer.

5. *Evaluation is done with a qualitative view.* Receiving a mark of 80% or a letter grade, such as a C, on a piece of writing does not give the writer any insight into his/her writing. It does not reveal the strengths or the weaknesses of the piece. It does not help the writer to become a better writer. Writers can only become better writers by knowing what they did well in a piece of writing and by finding out how to develop their strengths. If a school system does demand that a letter grade be given, then it should only be given in conjunction with feedback on the strengths of the piece.

6. *A multi-dimensional and developmental view is incorporated as it pertains to writing evaluation.* In order for evaluation of writing to be effective and of consequence, several pieces of writing written over time and written for a variety of purposes need to be used to form the evaluation. We know that time, a variety of writing experiences, and an amount of practice need to be considered in order for evaluation to be comprehensive. There is something in the old adage that ''practice makes perfect.'' Children exposed to a new genre will not use it as effectively as they will after they have had time to think about it and have had practice and experience using it. Pieces of writing chosen specifically for evaluation purposes should be ones that the writer feels confident about and has had the time, experience, and practice to perfect. Dated work samples give students, teachers, and parents an appreciation for the student's learning and his/her development as a writer. These dated work samples should be kept in a folder, which might be called the Growth Folder. The Growth Folder can contain several kinds

of writing. It may hold several pieces of finished writing and some pieces where the final writing product and all its drafts are included.

7. *Both the students and the teachers need to have a part in the evaluation process.* For too long, the role of the evaluation of writing was solely the responsibility of the teacher. In order for students to take responsibility for their writing, they need to become reflective about their writing. When the evaluation comes as a result of collaboration between student and teacher, both will learn more about the writer and the writing. If there is a positive community of writers in the classroom, students can be invited to evaluate not only their own work but the work of their peers, based on the positive strengths found in these writings. When the evaluation becomes the responsibility of teacher, student, and peers, much is learned by everyone; insights missed by one might be found by another. Evaluation as a collaborative process results in learning by everyone.

8. *Parents are a part of the evaluation process.* More and more, parents are being invited to be involved in the evaluation process. Having parents involved in the writing evaluation presents an opportunity for teachers to help parents understand the writing process so parents can develop a better appreciation for what their child is trying to do. When parents are involved, then the students can see they have many supports for their writing. A sample of a form for inviting parental input in writing and reading can be found in the Blackline Masters (Parent's Observation form).

Evaluation that Embraces the Shifts in Thinking about Writing

Because of the changes discussed in the previous pages there are changes in what we evaluate in writing and how we evaluate.

I. Evaluation and/or Reflection on Process

The writing process involves three stages: the getting ready to write stage (the gathering, aligning and rehearsal of ideas), the actual writing stage (creation of meaning), and the revising (shaping of meaning) and editing stage (polishing of meaning). Writers know these stages are not discrete and linear but tend to be blurry; writers move back and through these stages as the need arises. One aspect of evaluating the writing should involve looking at the ways in which the writer moves through the stages in order to complete a piece of writing. Observing the behaviors or strategies children exhibit as they write gives insights as to what needs to happen in order for the writer to grow and develop in his/her writing skills. At this point, it is important to understand that there is no ''right'' way to move through these stages. By observing the writer's actions, we can ascertain what behaviors have a positive effect on the writing and what behaviors might be a hindrance in producing a ''good'' piece.

1. Getting Ready to Write

Various words or phrases have been used to describe this stage, such as rehearsal, generating of ideas, gathering and collecting of ideas, and percolating. The terminology is descriptive and gives us an idea of what it means to get ready to write. During this stage, the following questions can be asked in order to gain insight and to evaluate how the writer writes.

a) Does the writer take the time necessary to gather ideas — through reflection, through discussions, through brainstorming, and/or by jotting down ideas?

b) Is the writer open to ideas and suggestions by others?

c) Does the writer organize his/her ideas through categorizing, webbing, or some other method of organizing?

d) Does the writer select the genre or design that will best shape his/her making of meaning?

e) Is the writer comfortable in trying out a number of leads or titles? A good beginning helps to ensure a good piece.

2. **Writing or Drafting Stage**

During this stage, we are hoping to see an uninhibited flow of ideas from the writer. At this time, there should be an emphasis on getting ideas down on paper without a concern for revision or a concern for mechanics, such as spelling or punctuation. The following questions might be asked.

a) Does the writer sit down and begin with confidence and sense of purpose?

b) Does the writer put more emphasis on getting ideas down in early drafts *and* more emphasis on connection of ideas in later drafts?

c) Is the writer confident enough to include ideas that in the initial stage may not seem to be applicable; that is, is the writer willing to play with ideas?

3. **Revising and Editing Stage**

This final stage involves ordering and connecting the ideas so that the piece will say what the writer wants it to say and so that it will be clear and coherent for the intended audience. At this time, spelling is checked for accuracy and punctuation is checked for appropriateness. The following questions may be asked.

a) Is the writer willing to take the time and effort required to polish the piece?

b) Does the piece say what the author wanted it to say in the way the author wanted it to be said? (Message and design concerns)

c) Does the writer know how to revise and edit by using a computer or, if not that fortunate, does he/she know about leaving a space between the lines large enough so that changes can be made right on the draft? Does the writer know about the use of arrows, carats, etc. for making changes?

d) Does the writer take care with spelling, punctuation and grammar so that the meaning is not clouded by faulty mechanics, form, or structure?

II. Self Monitoring of the Writer's Process and Product

These questions will help the writer monitor his/her writing process:

1. Is this a topic I am interested in? What do I hope to accomplish by writing this piece?

2. How do I gather my information for writing?

3. How did I choose my form to convey the meaning of the piece? Am I aware of the many forms for organizing meaning, such as story, poetry patterns, essay formats, comparison pieces, biography and autobiography designs, and letter format, to name just a few?

4. If I had difficulty in writing a good beginning, did I try the strategy of quickly writing three or four beginnings and then selecting the best one?

5. Did I encounter some problems in writing this piece? If so, what were they and how did I solve them? Did I ask someone to conference with me? Did I go back and gather more information? Did I search out other pieces like mine to see what

other writers did?

6. Was I open to suggestions from other people?

7. Did I take the time and effort needed to revise and edit my writing so that it says what I wanted to say in the way I wanted it to be said?

8. Did I consider my intended audience by giving them enough information so they could easily understand what I was trying to say?

9. Did I take care to use standard spelling, grammar, and punctuation out of deference to my audience so that these surface features would enhance my message?

10. Did I read the piece aloud to someone so I could hear how it sounds?

11. How do I ensure that I have something to write about tomorrow?

The following questions are some that a writer might ask about his or her finished piece of writing:

1. What am I trying to say? What is the most important thing and what are the less important things I am trying to say?

2. Does the piece make sense?

3. Should I expand on some parts and/or delete others?

4. Could I say some parts in a better way or another way?

5. Do I like the piece? What are its strengths?

6. Has the piece been polished (edited) so that no surface features, such as incorrect spelling or punctuation, mar the meaning?

7. Does the piece have a clear sense of purpose?

8. Will my intended audience feel the purpose of the piece has been accomplished?

III. Evaluation of the Product

Teachers have evaluated finished pieces of writing for a long time but often without criteria for doing so. Often a piece was read and compared to the writing of another student. The following can be used as a criteria for evaluating a finished piece of writing, by the teachers, by the writer and by a peer.

1. **Criteria for Evaluation**

    1.) Does the piece show a clear sense of purpose?

    2.) Is the meaning clear?

    3.) Does the piece have voice? That is, does the piece demonstrate the writer's sense of having something important to say, and is it said in a way that is particular to that writer?

    4.) Is the purpose and the meaning of the piece clear to the intended audience as well as to the writer?

    5.) Is the language selected appropriate to the piece? For example, if the piece is about a particular sport, then the terminology used must be common knowledge to the intended readers. The language used and the way it is used differ greatly when one considers the writing of a newspaper story compared to the writing of a love poem.

    6.) Is the design, genre, or grammar of the piece appropriate to the meaning that is being constructed?

    7.) Is the piece exciting, thought-provoking, and/or interesting?

If a letter grade or a numerical grade must be given due to outside constraints, then each item could be assigned a numerical weighting regarded as appropriate for the piece. Students could be told ahead of the actual writing time what the evaluation criteria will be and what the weighting is. If criteria is established for obtaining the evaluation mark ''A'' and every child in the class meets that criteria, then they all should be assigned the letter ''A'' on their evaluation records.

Writing Observation Cards — Teachers should use a large recipe card to keep dated observations of the child's writing process and of finished pieces. The observation comments can be based on the preceding monitoring questions. Students should become reflective of their writing process and evaluate their finished work. These reflections can be recorded by the student on their own observation card.

Three Strengths and a Wish

Several years ago Jerome Harste introduced us to a strategy for evaluation called Strengths and a Wish. This is a very worthwhile strategy for use by both the writer and by the teacher. When the writer uses this strategy, it forces the writer to look critically at his/her writing and to look at it in terms of strengths. Many writers are so very critical about their writing that they give themselves no credit for what they do well; they can only see their shortcomings. When ''three strengths and a wish'' is used, writers are forced to look at their writing in a positive vein and to look for what they want to do better in a future piece. By the same token, when a teacher looks at a student's writing, the teacher's forced to look for strengths and to focus on only one area in which to improve in the next piece of writing. This is a wonderful tool for evaluation, as it tends to motivate the writer to continue writing in the future, which has to be a goal of any teacher of writing. It also is a valuable strategy for a student to use when evaluating another student's writing. It forces other students to become reflective about what is good in a piece of writing.

Writing Interview

In order to get further insights into the student's view of writing, the following interview might be given.

Writing Interview

Name _____ Age _____ Grade _____

This interview is to gather information about writing as a construction-of-meaning process.

1. How do you pick a topic to write about?
2. How do you gather information in order to get ready for writing?
3. How do you insure a good beginning for your piece?
4. What do you do when you are writing and you don't know what to say next?
5. What do you do if you have a problem with what to write in the next piece?
6. Who do you know who is a good writer? What do you like about that person's writing?
7. What do you like about your writing?
8. What would you like to improve in your writing?
9. What would you say is the easiest thing about writing?
10. What would you say is the most difficult thing about writing?
11. Are you a good writer? How do you know?
12. If you were to teach someone how to write, what are some things you would say that you think would be helpful to that learner?

The evaluation tools just discussed are meant to act as a basis for writing evaluation. It is hoped that teachers will regard these strategies as a springboard to developing other strategies unique to their own classrooms and what they are trying to do.

Spelling Evaluation

Children learn to speak by progressive approximation towards standard speech. Water starts at "wa," becomes "wa wa," then "wader," and finally the child says "water."

Children learning to spell will learn by progressive approximation toward standard spelling.

In both learning to spell and learning to speak, overemphasis upon correct form inhibits learning.

Spelling Evaluation
Dew yew no how much I way?
"Isn't spelling fun" you sey
Theigh make a rule,
But I'm such a fule
That I break it every tyme.

Spelling Stages

Spelling, as described in *Spelling for Whole Language Classrooms* by Ethel Buchanan, is seen as a developmental process. The child learns to spell in the same way he learns all things: by progressive approximations toward standard form. The child makes a series of hypotheses or explanations as to how spelling works. The teacher, in evaluating the child, must discover which of these explanations of how "spelling works" the child is currently working on, so that he or she can help the child build his or her understanding of spelling.

Three of the major hypotheses (explanations about spelling) that a child uses are:

1. *Phonetic Hypothesis*

   This is sometimes referred to as the letter-naming hypothesis because the child believes that you spell according to the way you shape your mouth and tongue while producing letters of the alphabet. For example, the *c* in *cat* is often written as *k*, or the *w* in *watch* is often written as *y* because those letters are produced by the mouth and tongue in the fashion. Try it yourself by saying aloud *"cat"* and *"k."* See how your mouth and tongue are shaped similarly in *k* and at the beginning of *cat*. See how your mouth and tongue are shaped in *y* and at the beginning of *watch*. When the child is using this phonetic hypothesis, he/she will often spell *you are* as *u r*. It will do little good for a teacher at that point to say "No, it is spelled *you are*" as that information will not be accommodated in the child's working explanation of how spelling works.

2. *Phonic Hypothesis*

   The child will eventually begin to shift his main spelling strategy to rules about sound/symbol relationships. The child may begin this stage by seeing that certain sounds cannot be located by saying the alphabet. For example a six-year-old once said "I can't find oy and I have been through the whole alphabet." The child begins to discover sound/symbol rules such as that the "cuh" sound at the end of a one-syllable word is often spelled by using the letters *ck*, or an *e* at the end of a word makes the previous vowel say its name. At this stage it is easy to understand a child's writing for even though there may be many misspellings, the word can be "sounded out." These misspellings should be referred to as functional spellings, that is spellings that allow and encourage the child to function as an author. You will also quickly come to see that under pressure, a child will often revert back to a previously successful strategy, such as the phonetic hypothesis.

3. *Semantic Hypothesis*

Many adult poor spellers remain locked in the phonic hypothesis. Phonic rules are numerous, and there are so many exceptions to the rules that the phonic hypothesis eventually breaks down in its inconsistencies. Spelling in English is more predictable semantically (from meaning) than from rules of sound/symbol relationships. Good spelling requires the understanding of the various morphemes (smallest unit of meaning such as root, prefix or suffix) and word families (there is a "b" on the end of bomb because *bombard* has a similar meaning and the "*b*" is obvious in *bombard*). Again, a speller will often revert to a previously successful spelling strategy under pressure. As well, although good spellers use the semantic hypothesis as their predominant strategy, they will at times also use one of the earlier strategies. The spelling stages flow into one another, and a child's spelling efforts must be seen as a dynamic changing process rather than as a lockstep process.

Pre-Phonetic Spelling

In their earliest spelling strategies, children have not yet reached an understanding of spelling which centers on phonetics. This pre-phonetic stage will pass through a predictable developmental pattern.

a) *Scribble Stage.*

b) *Drawing Stage.* The child will use pictures.

c) *Negotiation Stage.* The child will use a combination of pictures, letters and numbers to portray meaning.

d) *Object Feature Stage.* The child will use symbols to portray people or objects. The larger or more important or more scary an object, the larger will be the print or the greater the number of symbols used to represent that object.

e) *Word Hypothesis Stage.* One or more symbols per word are used by the child.

f) *Syllabic Hypothesis Stage.* One symbol per syllable is used by the child.

g) *Alphabetic Hypothesis Stage.* More than one symbol per syllable is used by the child.

Pre-Phonetic Spelling
Placement Form

1. Have the student write his/her own name at the top of the page.
2. Write a sentence like this:

   > I live with my mom and dad in a beautiful house.

Observations

    a) Is the child's name spelled correctly?

    b) Does the child use only letters to spell words?

    c) Are *mom* and *dad* spelled with the same number of symbols?

    d) Does the child use one or more symbols per word?

    e) Does *beautiful* have more than one symbol?

    f) Is there more than one symbol per syllable?

    g) Does the child have the correct beginning letter for *mom*, *dad*, and *beautiful*?

    h) Does the child have the correct beginning letter for *with* or *house*?

Discussion of the Pre-Phonetic Spelling Placement Form

    a) Is the child's name spelled correctly?

       Correct spelling of the child's name indicates exposure to writing and spelling through sharing with a literate older person.

    b) Does the child use only letters to spell words?

       If only letters are used by the child, then the child has probably passed the negotiation stage.

    c) Are *mom* and *dad* spelled with the same number of symbols?

       If *dad* has more symbols than *mom* or is written with larger letters, then the child is probably at the object feature stage.

    d) Does the child use one or more symbol per word?

       If the child has at least one symbol per word, the child is

probably at the word hypothesis stage.

e) Does *beautiful* have more than one symbol?

If *beautiful* has two or three symbols, the child is likely at the syllabic hypothesis stage.

f) Is there more than one symbol per syllable?

If there is more than one symbol per syllable, the child is likely at the alphabetic hypothesis stage.

g) Does the child have the correct beginning letter for *mom, dad,* and *beautiful?*

If the child starts *mom, dad* and *beautiful* with *m, d* and *b,* the child is likely at the early phonetic stage, as these are phonetic letters.

h) Does the child have the correct beginning letter for *with* or *house?*

If the child starts the words *with* and *house* with *w* and *h,* the child has some knowledge of phonic generalizations, as *h* and *w* are phonic letters, letters with sound/symbol relationships.

Spelling Placement Test

In the Spelling Placement Test, words have been chosen that will help teachers to decide which stage of spelling development a student is in. As in reading, it is the child's miscues that give us insight into the spelling hypothesis he/she is using.

In words 1-10 — the focus is on the initial consonants which are all phonetic consonants.

In words 11, 12 and 13 — the focus is on the short vowels to see if the child is using phonetic or phonic generalizations.

In words 14, 15, 16 and 17 — the test is on the initial consonant *g, c, h,* and *w,* which are consonants that are not phonetic. The child has to have some knowledge of letter/sound relationships (phonics) in order to predict the letter that goes with the word starting with *w*, *h*, and the hard sound of *c* and *g*.

In the words for 18 — the test is to see if the preconsonant nasalized letter is written in by the child. Children in the phonetic stage omit this letter.

In the words for 19 — these are commonly used words that are not phonetic or phonic but, if spelled correctly, indicate an interest in spelling.

In words 20 through 50 — these words have been chosen to test phonic generalizations, such as *ar, ow, oi, ck*.

In words 51-100 — the semantic hypothesis is being tested to see if the students have knowledge of prefixes, suffixes and root words needed to successfully spell these words.

Spelling Placement Test

1. me	1. no	1. so
2. dog	2. dig	2. dad
3. mat	3. man	3. mop
4. rat	4. run	4. rag
5. bad	5. bag	5. big
6. name	6. nap	6. not
7. top	7. tip	7. tin
8. pot	8. pat	8. pan
9. frog	9. fat	9. free
10. kiss	10. keep	10. kit
11. pet	11. set	11. met
12. sit	12. pit	12. fit
13. fat	13. bat	13. rat
14. goat	14. game	14. go
15. cat	15. call	15. come
16. hit	16. help	16. home
17. watch	17. water	17. wand
18. jump	18. bump	18. pump
19. the	19. is	19. was
20. bar	20. car	20. far
21. hate	21. spade	21. shade
22. my	22. try	22. sky
23. toy	23. boy	23. joy
24. now	24. cow	24. bow
25. green	25. seen	25. teen
26. tick	26. truck	26. puck
27. skate	27. slice	27. slime
28. walking	28. talking	28. pulling
29. coat	29. boat	29. toad
30. when	30. where	30. why

Spelling Placement Test

31. stand	31. still	31. stamp
32. they	32. because	32. does
33. boot	33. toot	33. root
34. jolly	34. funny	34. pretty
35. drape	35. dress	35. drip
36. dew	36. flew	36. stew
37. work	37. worth	37. worm
38. giant	38. germ	38. gentle
39. right	39. light	39. fight
40. quiet	40. queen	40. quit
41. steam	41. leaf	41. mean
42. making	42. riding	42. hiding
43. running	43. winning	43. shopping
44. found	44. sound	44. round
45. coin	45. oil	45. soil
46. nation	46. station	46. fraction
47. enough	47. tough	47. rough
48. knee	48. knock	48. wrong
49. manage	49. garbage	49. cabbage
50. church	50. chicken	50. children
51. crafts	51. bomb	51. sign
52. worked	52. walked	52. talked
53. wanted	53. started	53. sounded
54. northerly	54. elderly	54. easterly
55. childish	55. foolish	55. whitish
56. survey	56. surmount	56. surname
57. happier	57. prettier	57. funnier
58. recall	58. regain	58. remember
59. contrary	59. contraband	59. contradict
60. Spain	60. England	60. France

61. girl's	61. boy's	61. cat's
62. boys'	62. girls'	62. dogs'
63. national	63. natural	63. extremity
64. competition	64. explanation	64. inclination
65. medicine	65. revision	65. gradual
66. dishonest	66. dishonour	66. disgust
67. irresistible	67. irregular	67. irrational
68. predict	68. prefer	68. predate
69. death	69. health	69. breadth
70. company	70. fallacy	70. truancy
71. sorrowful	71. hopeful	71. mournful
72. redness	72. fullness	72. greatness
73. children's	73. mice's	73. oxen's
74. peerless	74. fearless	74. painless
75. obstruct	75. observe	75. obstacle
76. submit	76. subside	76. subsoil
77. violinist	77. flutist	77. receptionist
78. transmit	78. transport	78. transgress
79. civilize	79. colonize	79. economize
80. conception	80. perception	80. deception
81. gesture	81. creature	81. picture
82. unnecessary	82. unnatural	82. unnoticed
83. identical	83. historical	83. topical
84. philosopher	84. phonograph	84. telephone
85. authoress	85. giantess	85. lioness
86. pleasure	86. photography	86. introduction
87. illegal	87. irregular	87. illiterate
88. biology	88. sociology	88. criminology
89. toxic	89. dramatic	89. mimic
90. docile	90. fragile	90. tactile
91. homicide	91. suicide	91. genocide

92. sympathy	92. syllable	92. symmetry
93. atheism	93. barbarism	93. organism
94. mathematics	94. ethics	94. graphics
95. uncomplaining	95. uncommitted	95. uncomfortable
96. predictable	96. predetermined	96. precise
97. polygon	97. polygraph	97. polyester
98. foreshadow	98. foreground	98. foretell
99. studious	99. melodious	99. odious
100. exonerate	100. exquisite	100. exorbitant

Spelling Placement Test Explanation

This test is designed to generate material that can be used to look for the specific spelling strategies that a child is using. The child's spelling miscues provide more interesting and more valuable knowledge than words that are spelled correctly.

Points to ponder before you use this test:

1. This test, like all tests, gives you but a reflection of your child's thinking. Used by itself it may give you insights into what the child thinks spelling is all about, but it will never accurately reflect all that the child knows about spelling. It is best used as one of many observations and recordings about how the child uses the spelling process.

2. Words on the spelling list *can be and should be changed to meet the specific circumstances* of your child's spelling environment. There is nothing sacred about the words selected except that they try to generate material on some aspect of spelling. For example the *OW* phonic rule or use of phonetic generalizations to spell the first letter of a word correctly, or use of a specific root, prefix, or suffix.

3. There is nothing stopping you from saying that a child who spells 33 of the 100 words correctly is at a 3.3 spelling level. That number will be completely meaningless as this test is not, and

should not be, standardized. But if you do need to generate numbers, this test will usually generate high ones, so at least it will be to the advantage of the child.

4. The three lists of 100 words are similar in regard to the aspects of spelling that they focus on.

> For example Number 60 on each test *Spain, England,* and *France* each look to see if the child has formed a hypothesis for capitalization of the first letter of proper nouns.

> For example Number 44 of each test *found, sound,* and *round* all look at the phonic generalization of *OUND.*

The tests can be used three times a year: The first one on initial entry, the second midyear, and the third at the end of the year. When you use the test material for analyzing the child's generation of spelling miscues and not simply for counting the number of words spelled correctly, you will have some measurement of the growth and development of the child's "thinking about spelling" or his/her "use of the spelling process."

5. The first sentence, "I live with my mom and dad in a beautiful house." could be used with early spellers, such as four- or five-year-old children.

The observations you will make on the generated script will help you see what spelling strategies the child is using at a prephonetic stage. (For a further explanation of these early stages, see Spelling for Whole Language Classrooms by Ethel Buchanan.) If the child shows evidence of using phonetic strategies, the spelling placement test can be given in addition to the above sentence.

6. In using the spelling placement form, always dictate far more words than the child can spell correctly. Remember, it is the spelling miscues that are generated that have the most value, because they help us understand the child's view of the spelling process. For young children, it is usually inappropriate to

dictate the whole list, as they will become frustrated. Dictate enough words to generate a sampling of miscues with which to work.

Following the placement test, you may wish to note interesting miscues on the following form. This is optional, as the observations may be placed right on the test paper if that works better for you. If you use the form, five to ten miscues should be enough to draw a conclusion as to the spelling strategies the child is predominantly using.

Example #	Test #	Test	Script	Observation
1	36	DEW	DOO	Choosing incorrect phonic rule
2	38	GIANT	JIANT	Using phonetic strategy for "J"
3	41	STEAM	STEME	Using incorrect phonic rule Incorrect vowel marker
4	43	RUNNING	RUNING	Not applying correct syntactic rule
5	44	FOUND	FOWND	Using incorrect phonic rule
6	45	COIN	KOIN	Using phonetic strategy for "K"
7	49	MANAGE	MANEGE	Using incorrect phonic rule
8	51	CRAFTS	CRAFS	Not using semantics clues
9	52	WORKED	WORKET	Not applying correct syntax rule
10	54	NORTHERLY	NORTHERNLY	Using wrong morphemic unit

Conclusions

The student's dominant strategies are phonic. Phonetic strategies remain partially in use. Syntactic/semantic strategies are emerging.

SPELLING MISCUE OBSERVATION

Student Name _____   **Room** _____

Observation Date _____

Miscue #	Text Item #	TEXT	SCRIPT	OBSERVATION
1.				
2.				
3.				
4.				
5.				
6.				
7.				
8.				
9.				
10.				

Conclusion
(reflection, spelling stage) _____

_____

_____

_____

_____

CLASS SUMMARY OF
SPELLING MISCUE OBSERVATIONS

NB Use different color ink to record each date's observations.

Teacher _____

Date _____

Date _____

Date _____

Date _____

	Pre-Phonetic				Early Phonetic			Advanced Phonetic			Phonic			Syntactic -Semantic	
	Not yet apparent	Emerging	Dominant Strategy	Remains partially in use	Emerging	Dominant Strategy	Remains partially in use	Emerging	Dominant Strategy	Remains partially in use	Emerging	Dominant Strategy	Remains partially in use	Emerging	
_____															
_____															
_____															
_____															
_____															
_____															
_____															
_____															
_____															
_____															
_____															
_____															
_____															
_____															
_____															
_____															
_____															
_____															
_____															
_____															
_____															
_____															

Some examples from the Spelling Placement Test with Accompanying Observations

TEXT

I LIVE WITH MY MOM AND DAD IN A BEAUTIFUL HOUSE

This is an example of a pre-phonetic child who is using pictures to convey meaning. The *i* shows that she is just starting to see a role for print in her symbolic representation of meaning.

The child is at a stage of spelling development where she uses pictorial representation as her main strength for making meaning with print.

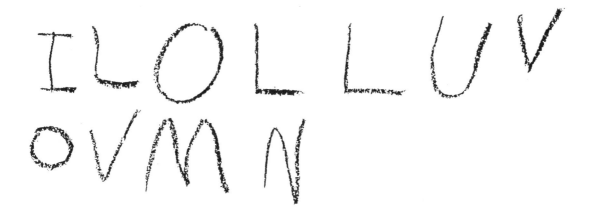

TEXT

I LIVE WITH MY MOM AND DAD IN A BEAUTIFUL HOUSE

This child uses one symbol for each word. These symbols tend to be of a limited number and to be repeated at this developmental stage.

The child is at a pre-phonetic stage of spelling development, where she uses one letter per word to represent meaning.

ILWM MOMADA D
EABHOWS

TEXT
  I LIVE WITH MY MOM AND DAD IN A BEAUTIFUL HOUSE

This child still often uses only one letter per word. That letter tends to be a phonetic choice in many instances. For example the *i* in the word *in* is spelled with an *e*. The shape of the mouth and tongue in the short *i* and the long *e* closely correspond. The child also shows a sight knowledge of the common words *MOM* and *DAD*. This denotes a growing awareness in the child of standard spellings. *HOUSE* is spelled *HOWS* by the child. This shows that the child is beginning to be aware of some phonic generalizations.

The child appears to be at a phonetic stage of spelling development.

More interesting information may be gained by dictating to this child the first part of a spelling placement list. (See next spelling sample.)

ME

DOG HAT

DOG
MAT
RAT
BAD
NAMe

TOP
GAT Jet
FAG frog
KEA ← kiss the

PAT pet

SAT sit

GOT goat
HAT CAT hate
SLR star
HAT hit
GAP jump
NKO now
O MI my
TOK
WOA watch
GN green
EC SCT tick/scate
TE
WEN walking
LOT coat
SAD stand

Sample on previous page.

This spelling sample indicates that the child is at the phonetic stage of spelling development. This child's spelling miscues provide a wealth of insights into how the spelling process is being used and how he/she thinks spelling goes together. It is exciting to look at each miscue.

1.	NAME	NAM	Not using final E as a vowel sound control
2.	JET	ᒐAT	Reversal of the letter J
			(Heavens, could this kindergarten child be showing early signs of dyslexia?)
			The student has put the letter A for the short E in JET which shows the phonetic hypothesis or letter naming strategy
3.	PET	PAT	Perfect example of using the phonetic vowel replacement
4.	GOAT	GOT	Not using a second vowel as a vowel sound control
5.	JUMP	ᒐAP	Preconsonant nasalized, M is missing as it is expected to be missing in the phonetic hypothesis.
			(Horrors, there is that reverse J again)

How much better we can understand the child and how he views the spelling process by skillfully observing his spelling miscues than by noting he has seven correct words.

How do you help ''seven correct words''. Helping a child in the phonetic stage is easy and fun. (See *Spelling for the Whole Language Classroom,* by Ethel Buchanan).

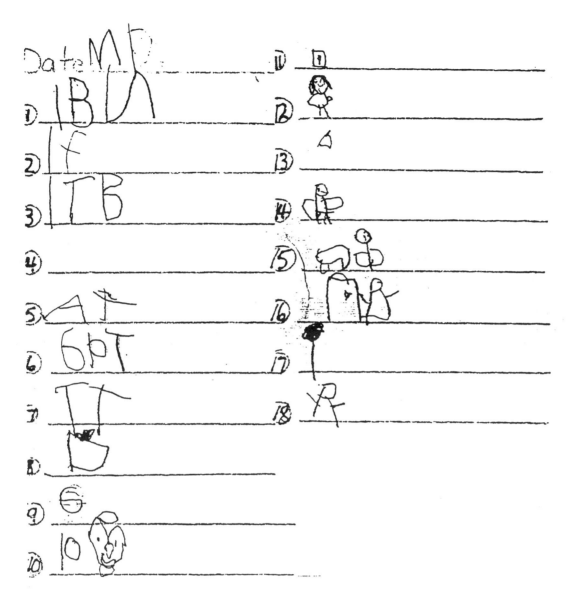

This sample shows the early Grade One child to be using a random but limited string of letters for representation of words. As the pressure of the dictation builds, the child reverts back to a previous spelling strategy of pictorial representation.

This reversion to a previous spelling strategy when spelling becomes difficult for a child is very common. It illustrates the limitations of any dictated test situation, including the use of this spelling placement test. No single source of data gives you a complete picture of the child's progress. Each source shows us one piece of the intriguing puzzle of a child's ongoing development.

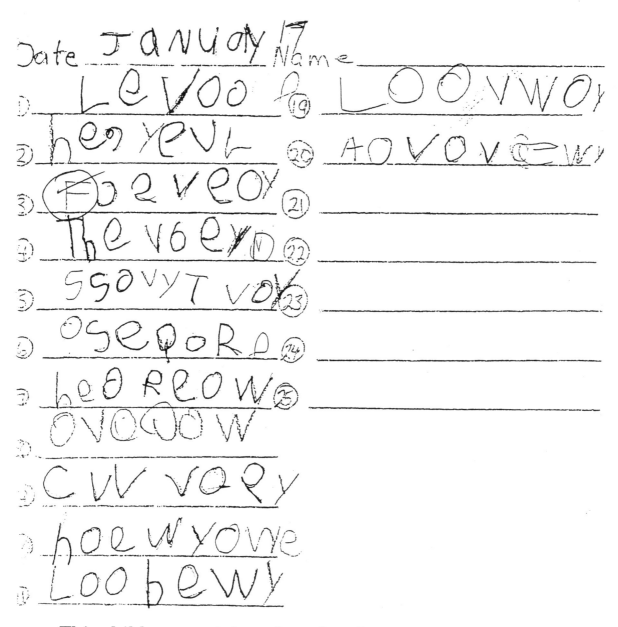

This child uses a string of random letters as a spelling strategy. Usually seven or eight letters are used per word.

This sample is also a clear example of the danger of using only one sample of language in one language situation to judge a student. This activity, a dictated list of unrelated words, obviously had little purpose or meaning for the child. Under these conditions, we see something quite different than we see in the next example where we see the *same* child in a more meaningful and purposeful language activity *one day later.*

January 18

TEXT

I am MAD
BKs SSW s To BT UP
MY sdllry.

I AM MAD
BECAUSE SOMEONE WANTS TO BEAT UP
MY SISTER

This example shows a child clearly using a phonetic hypothesis as his major spelling strategy.

N.B. This strategy was generated by the child looking into a mirror and drawing himself and then writing about how he was feeling in the picture he drew.

* Idea and samples come from Susan Bukta who was a Grade One teacher at Shaughnessy Park School in Winnipeg, Manitoba.

```
1. Me ✓              20. Jump ✓        Spelling
2. dog ✓             21. naw ✓           31. is ✓
3. Mat ✓             22. My ✓            32. Boot ✓
4. rat ✓                                 33. Jrape
5. Bad ✓             23. Boy             34. gu
6. Name ✓            24. woch            35. rit
7. top ✓             25. Green ✓         36. kyit
8. Jet ✓             26. Tik             37. Steme ✓
9. Frog ✓            27. skase           38. Making ✓
10. kiss ✓           28. Walking ✓       39. running ✓
11. The ✓            29. cot             40. fund
12. pet ✓            30. sand
13. sit ✓
14. hat ✓                26
15. goat ✓
16. hate ✓
17. Cat ✓
18. Stor
19. hit ✓
```

This is an illustration from an older student. The fact that there are twenty-six words spelled correctly tells us little. There is more interesting information in the spelling miscues.

	#	TEXT	SCRIPT	OBSERVATION
1.	33	DRAPE	JRAPE	Confusing D and J is very common in children whose ancestral language may not contain separate sounds for D and J as in the case of this student.
2.	35	RIGHT	RIT	This student uses phonic rules at times but has not yet mastered IGHT. At this time he reverts back to a phonetic strategy.
3.	37	STEAM	STEME	Darn, picked the wrong vowel control marker — definitely trying to apply phonic rules.

This student in this sample appears to be in a middle phonic stage of spelling development. Note as well that phonetic strategies remain partially in use.

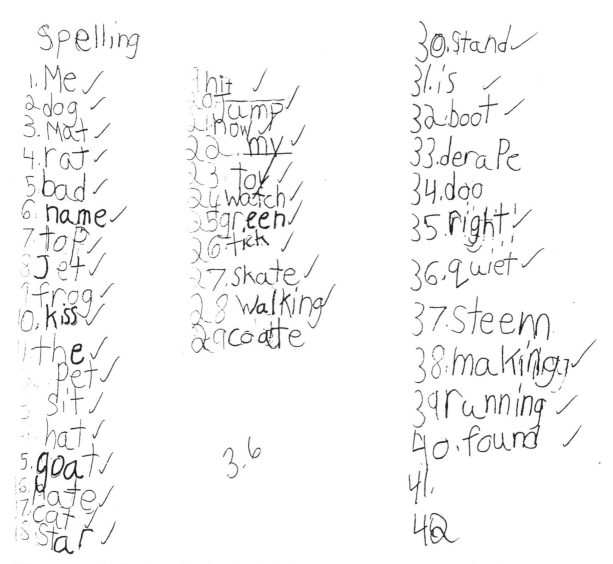

This sample had to be included just to see some wonderful miscues.

	#	TEXT	SCRIPT	OBSERVATION
1.	33	DRAPE	DERAPE	You can almost hear the child sounding this word out to herself.
2.	34	DEW	DOO	Well it worked in TOO, didn't it?
3.	37	STEAM	STEEM	Darn, wrong vowel sound control marker again.

This also shows an example in which the teacher stopped dictating far too soon. The miscues were just getting interesting. It is through a child's spelling miscues that we can see how his/her mind views the spelling process.

2.5

Sentence — <u>I live with my mom and dad in a beteful</u>
<u>house.</u>

me ✓	green ✓	wontid id for ed
dog ✓	tic omitted k	joly ll
mat ✓	skat(e) omitted e	
rat ✓	waking silent l	
bad ✓	cote oa	
name ✓	stand ✓	
top ✓	is ✓	
Jet ✓	boot ✓	
frog ✓	drake k for p	
kiss ✓	do dew	
the ✓	rite right	
pet ✓	quit et	
sit ✓	stem ea	
hat ✓	makeing drop e	
gote goat	runing double n	
hate ✓	fund ou	
cat ✓	coen e for i	
star ✓	nashn shn for tion	
hit ✓	enenuf	
jump ✓	nie	
naw a for o	mang	
my ✓	thaiy	
toy ✓	crafs	
woch omitted t	work ed	

What wonderful miscues from which we can anticipate the path
of this child's future learning! By dictating more words, a wealth
of miscue information is given.

1. me
2. dog
3. mat
4. rat
5. bad
6. name
7. top
8. jet
9. frog
10. kiss
11. the
12. pat
13. sit
14. hat
15. goat
16. hate
17. cat
18. store
19. hit
20. jump
21. know
22. my
23. toy
24. watch
25. green

37 steam
38 making
39 running
40 found
41 coin
42 nation
43 enogh x
44 knee
45 manage
46 they
47 crafts
48 worked
49 wanted
50 jolly
51 northernly x
52 childish
53 work
54 happier
55 recoll
56 better
57 Spain
58 girls x
59 boys x
60 giant
61 perdict

73 consept x
74 gesture
75 uncessisary x
76 identical
77 fullasafur x
78 autheriest x
79 pleasure
80 elegal x
81 bioligy x
82 talksic x
83 fracyile
84 homeside x
85 simphy x
86 ourganism x
87 mathamatics x
88 uncomplaining
89 predictable
90 playg x

In this example, we see an older child well into the early semantic stage of spelling. Some of his/her needs are very apparent from his/her miscues.

1.	51	NORTHERLY	NORTHERNLY	Good thinking! Used a similar suffix.
2.	58	GIRLS	GIRL'S	Needs knowledge of possessives.
3.	59	BOYS	BOYS'	Needs knowledge of plural possessives.
4.	75	UNNECESSSARY	UNESSISARY	Needs greater understanding of how prefixes are added to roots. For examples of this see how this student spells words 75 and 80.
5.	77	PHILOSOPHER	FULLASAFUR	Reverting back to phonic approach as the difficulty increases.

Dictations of Writing Samples

The best source of material to evaluate children's progress in spelling is their own day-to-day writing. In a child's day-to-day conversation, we hear their oral language develop towards conventional standard language by progressive approximation toward the norm. In learning to say the word *water*, a child may first say ''wa.'' This attempt at meaning excites the parents. The parents' excitement encourages the child, especially when he/she can say ''wa'' and get a drink of water for saying it. When language is purposeful and functional, this is learned quickly. Later the child may say ''wawa'' for the word *water*. Again, the parents are excited at the child's progress toward standard language norms. Then the child may say ''wader.'' The parents are again pleased at their child's progress. It is interesting to note that at this point in the child's oral language development, the parents do *not* do any of the following:

   a) Tell the child ''No! It is not *wader*, it is *water*. Repeat after me one hundred times the word *water*. ''
   b) Check to see if Jenny down the street, who is the same age as their son, is already saying *water* and not *wader*.
   c) Think that their child will not eventually be able to say ''*water*'' correctly.

Parents believe their children will learn to speak. They compare each child's efforts at oral language against the child's own previous performance. They are excited by each progressive approximation toward the standard. They realize that *wawa* or *wader* are utterances that allow their child to function as a conversationalist. They do not expect a two-year-old to speak like a six-year-old. So, too, we should not expect a six-year-old child to spell like a twelve-year-old child.

Spelling is developmental in the same way oral language is: by progressive approximation toward standard spelling. The early spellings of a child (for example *BKWS* for *because*) are vital as they allow the young child to function as an author. By looking at a child's spelling miscues, we can see that child's progressive approximation in his/her journey toward standard spelling.

One very good way of obtaining a sample of this spelling development is to dictate a sample of his/her free writing.

Here are two samples, taken over time from a grade one student. The first was generated from her daily writing. The second is a dictation of the first sample. Note the obvious growth in spelling as the approximations move toward standard spelling.

	TEXT	SCRIPT 1	SCRIPT 2
A.	COLOR	CILR	COLAER
B.	DOLLAR	DAELRS	DALERS
C.	BIRTHDAY	BEENTHDAY	BERTHDAY

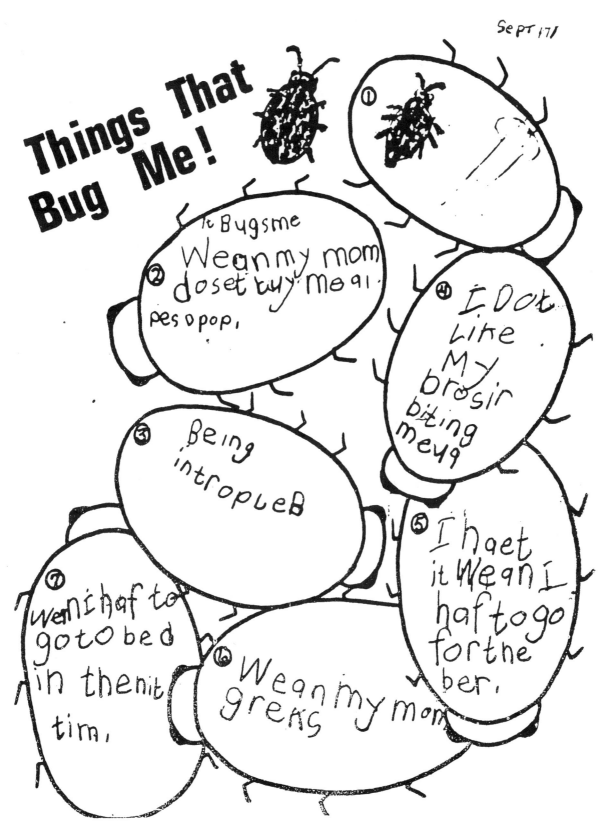

Sept 17/

Things That Bug Me!

①

② It Bugs me
Wean my mom
doset buy me a
pesopop,

④ I Dot
Like
My
brosir
biting
me ug

③ Being
intropueß

⑤ I haet
it Wean I
haf to go
for the
ber.

⑦ wen I haf to
go to bed
in the nit
tim,

⑥ Wean my mom
greks

Dictation of Child's Free Writing. Sample on page 104.

June, '1

It bugs me when ~~A~~ my mom doesnt
buy me a pizza pop,

being intaropted.

I don't like my brother ~~biting~~
beting me up,

I haet it when I have to go for
the beer,

when my mom drinks,

When I have to go to dbed
in the night time,

Discussion of Writing Sample - "Things That Bug Me"

Here we see an example of a child's free writing and that same script dictated ten months later. Both pieces generated some interesting miscues that could be analyzed on the spelling miscue observation form to determine the child's stage of spelling development. They can also be used in another valuable way. We can use them to look at the child's spelling growth through approximation toward standard spelling. We selected ten miscues in the first piece and observed their changes when the sample was dictated some nine months later.

	TEXT	SCRIPT 1	SCRIPT 2	
1.	WHEN	WEAN	WHEN	+
2.	DOESN'T	DOSET	DOESNT	+
3.	PIZZA POP	PESOPOP	PIZZA POP	+
4.	INTERRUPTED	INTROPIED	INTAROPTED	+
5.	BEATING	BITING	BETING	+
6.	HATE	HAET	HAET	N
7.	HAVE	HAF	HAVE	+
8.	BEER	BER	BEER	+
9.	DRINKS	GREKS	DRINKS	+
10.	NIGHT	NIT	NIGHT	+

In Script 1 (September), we see this student in a late phonetic stage of spelling development. In the June dictation, the student is solidly in the phonic level of spelling development.

In the right-hand column, we look at the child's spelling development to see if it is moving toward standard spelling. The "+" symbol indicates a move toward standard spelling. A "−" symbol indicates a move away from standard spelling and a letter *N* indicates no change. There are ten samples of miscues used in the first script. In nine of these items, the child has moved toward standard spelling on the dictation. We can then say that in this sample the child has moved toward standard spelling in 90% of the items.

This is a very positive way of looking at a child's developmental growth in spelling. It is easy to share this view of the child's progress with parents and to help the parents learn to recognize the value and power of a developmental view of children's learning.

Sample of Student's Free Writing

Dear Mr Cochrane
do you woke around the school with the vise prinsabol___. I think the vise prinsobol is verey nice ☐ yes or ☐ No. Wot are you going to be for holloween_____ I am going to be a Horker for Holloween And I mite go to the holloween dance at north wode.

god biy Mr Cochran

I hope you will have a good

Holloween !

Same Writing Dictated Eight Months Later

Dear Mr. Cocrin
do you wolk arownd with the vice prinsobol?___ I thing the vice prinsobol is very nice ☐ yes or ☐ no, wot are you going to be for Hollowen? _____ . I am going to be a Hocer for Holbwen. and I mit go to the Hollowen dancns at North wood.

good by Mr. Cocrin.

I hope you will have a good Hollowen.

— 108 —

Observation of Preceding Samples

Here is a marvelous example of a child's free writing and how a dictation at a later date can illustrate a child's growth in spelling through progressive approximation toward standard spelling forms.

FORM B

Student name _____   Room <u>8</u>

Observation Dates: 1st <u>October</u>

2nd <u>January</u>

	TEXT	SCRIPT 1	SCRIPT 2	SYMBOL
1.	WALK	WOKE	WALK	+
2.	VICE	VISE	VICE	+
3.	PRINCIPAL	PRINSOBUL	PRINSOBOL	N
4.	VERY	VEREY	VERY	+
5.	WHAT	WOT	WOT	+
6.	HOOKER	HORKER	HOCER	+
7.	WOOD	WODE	WOOD	+
8.	MIGHT	MITE	MIT	−
9.	GOOD	GOD	GOOD	+
10.	BYE	BIY	BY	+

Number of +'s = 7

7/10 x 100 = 70%

70% of the child's spelling miscues are moving toward, or have become, standard spelling.

Progressive Approximation Form

FORM B

% OF SPELLING MISCUES MOVING TOWARD STANDARD SPELLING

Student Name _____   Room _____

Observation Dates: 1st_____

2nd_____

	TEXT	SCRIPT 1	SCRIPT 2	SYMBOL
1.				
2.				
3.				
4.				
5.				
6.				
7.				
8.				
9.				
10.				

KEY TO SYMBOLS: + = moving toward standard spelling
N = no change
– = moving away from standard spelling

Number of +'s = __.

__/10 x 100 = __%

__% of the child's miscues are moving toward, or have become, standard spelling.

Spelling - Self-Evaluation

Often children know when they have misspelled a word. The following is a simple strategy to encourage children to evaluate their own spelling and to explore alternative spellings for words they are unsure of.

1. Have children go over their writing and circle the words they think they may have misspelled. Children will usually identify 80-90% of their spelling miscues.

2. Next, have them underline the part of the word they have misspelled. Again, the children will usually know which part of the word they are experiencing difficulty with. Usually the middle or ending of a word will be the trouble area.

3. Have children write several alternate possible spellings of the circled part of the word and to identify the one that looks right to them. This strategy is one that many adults use and can be taught to children at an early age.

Reporting to Parents

The teacher/student/parent conference and the report card are important parts of the evaluation process. In these areas we are beginning to see some major changes.

Traditionally, teachers were expected to *tell* the parents how their child was doing in school. It was a teacher-dominated interaction with very little input from the parents and no input from the student. We are now moving to a shared responsibility of evaluation in which parental input is invited and where students are required to reflect on their own progress. What a change from the days when students waited for their parents to come home from a parent teacher conference to tell them how they were doing. *"What did my teacher say about me?"* or *"How am I doing?"* or *"Will I pass?"* will become questions of the past.

In whole language, evaluation is more an exchange of information, in which teachers have input, parents share their observations and wishes, and students contribute through their self-evaluations.

So the model has moved from

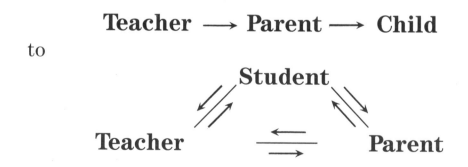

Teacher ⟶ Parent ⟶ Child

to

We will provide suggestions as to how each of the three participants may share information at the evaluation meeting. These are meant as guidelines for teachers to consider in structuring the evaluation conference and should be adapted to meet the individual needs of the classroom and those of the community involved.

Teacher's Role: The teacher's role in whole language evaluation is still a large one. The teacher will draw together samples of the student's work along with written observations about the child's work and efforts. Some sources of information are:
- bulk reading records
- samples of student's work
- anecdotal cards of ongoing assessments
- taped samples of the child's oral reading
- video tapings
- tests
- Reading Development Continuum placements

After the teacher has gathered this data together and has had some time to reflect on the information and time to think of the child's future learning, the next step is to conference with the student.

Student's Role: The student is expected to select pieces of work that he/she wishes to have used in the evaluation process and is also asked to reflect on his/her progress for the term. Some teachers have their students fill in a mock report that invites them to write on their progress for the term in each subject area. The students also comment on what they think their focus should be for the next term.

Parent's Role: Parents are invited to play a role in the evaluation process. Parents are asked to observe their children at home and to check off their observations on the sheet sent home at the beginning of the term. (See page 114) These observation sheets should be sent home early in the term so parents know what to observe. An additional sheet should be sent home about two weeks before the evaluation so parents can fill them in. The parents should bring these sheets to the evaluation conference. The parents are also invited to state their wishes in regard to their child's efforts in the next term.

Parent's Observation Form

	Mon.	Tues.	Wed.	Thurs.	Fri.	Week end
I Time spent at home:						
Reading to my child						
My child reading to me						
My child reading to himself/herself						
TOTAL						

II   My child's favorite book for me to read to him/her: _____

_____

III   Approximate number of times a week my child will write something at home: ___

_____

My child uses writing (e.g. to write thank you notes, telephone messages, letters to

friends and relatives, stories, etc.):_____

_____

IV   Three things my child likes to do at home: Please elaborate.

1. _____

2. _____

3 _____

V   Topics my child is very interested in: _____

_____

_____

VI   My child feels this way about reading and writing: _____

_____

_____

VII   My child tells me he/she likes to do this in school: _____

_____

_____

VIII   I feel the school does this well: _____

_____

_____

IX   I would like to know more about: _____

_____

_____

The Teacher and Student Evaluation Conference

This conference should take place before the report card is written. This is the time when an open dialogue takes place between the teacher and the student regarding the student's progress based on the data that both the teacher and student have brought to the conference. The dialogue should also include teacher and student reflections on the past term. The student should have the opportunity to present his/her assessment first and then the teacher should offer his/hers. After both parties have presented their assessments, further discussion should take place regarding any differences in perceptions. Also at this time, the teacher and student will determine a plan for the student's learning for the next term. A rough draft of the report card ends the conference. The final copy of the report card is done by the teacher and sent home before the teacher/student/parent conference so parents and their child have time to discuss the report card beforehand.

The Teacher/Student/Parent Conference

The teacher/student/parent conference should take place after the report card has been sent home. The student leads the conference by showing his/her parent(s) the work samples and tests that were used as a basis for assessment. The teacher can also share additional information. After a discussion about the work, the parent(s) can express their reaction to the work shown and to the final assessment on the report card. The parents then share their observations of their child at home. They can use the Parent's Observation sheet as a guide for their discussion of these observations.

The conference ends with a discussion by all parties concerning plans for the student's work in the next term. The teacher records these plans and gives one copy to the student and one to the parent(s).

With this system of evaluating and reporting, the student has a much larger role than before. It is hoped that by inviting the student to be active in the evaluating process, he/she will claim more ownership and responsibility for his/her learning. For parents it is a process that recognizes the impact that parents can and do have on the success of their child in school.

Teachers still have a very active role, but their job becomes more effective because of the active role played by parents and students. Evaluation has become a truly collaborative process.

End of the Year Records to pass on to the next year's teacher:

There are three things that are important to pass on to next year's teacher.

1. **A Portfolio of the Student's Writing**

Donald Graves pioneered this idea, and it has found instant acceptance with whole language teachers. There are now many interpretations of student portfolios.

Here is ours.

The students should select four or five pieces of writing to put in the portfolio. These should be finished, "published" (edited and polished) pieces that show what the student does best as a writer. Although the student may be encouraged by the teacher to display samples of different genres he/she has found success with, the final decision of what goes into the portfolio should be the child's. Some teachers would let the child include spelling tests or math speed tests. We would limit the items in the portfolio to samples of the student's authorship. The portfolio itself can be a file folder or a large sheet of folded art paper. The student may decorate and illustrate the folder with pride. Each year, four or five new pieces of writing are added to the portfolio. It is easy to see that in a few years a wonderful collection of the student's best work will be accumulated. How encouraging and motivating to be the owner of such a folder.

2. Student Resumés

Student resumés provide an excellent source of information about the student for the next year's teacher. The student has control of the information presented on the page. Often the "voice" of the child can be clearly "heard" from the writing on the resumé. Resumés are a great help to the teacher preparing for a new year. For teachers who like to write to the students in their classes prior to the beginning of the new school year, the resumé provides many ideas for making those letters meaningful and personal. On page 118 is an example of a resumé for use in elementary school for student use in kindergarten through to the end of Grade five. On page 119 is an example of a resumé for students of Grade six, seven and eight.

Student Resumé for Elementary School Students

Student Name _____

School _____

Grade _____ Room_____   Date _____

Birthdate: Month _____ Day _____ Year _____

The best thing I ever did in school was _____

_____

_____

_____

_____

I am _____

_____

_____

_____

I like _____

_____

_____

_____

I don't like _____

_____

_____

_____

My family _____

_____

_____

I would like to learn next year_____

_____

_____

_____

FORM I

_____
Student's Signature

Student Resumé for Going into Junior High

Student Name _____

Elementary School _____

Date _____

Birthdate: Month _____ Day _____ Year _____

Background Information (birthplace, family members) _____

_____

_____

_____

Elementary Career (interests, strengths, weaknesses) _____

_____

_____

_____

Personality (strengths, weaknesses) _____

_____

_____

_____

_____

Personal Goals (short term and long term) _____

_____

_____

_____

_____

Questions and Concerns about Junior High _____

_____

_____

_____

Expectations of Junior High _____

_____

_____

_____

FORM 2

_____

Student's Signature

3. A list of the student's ten favorite books read this year in order of preference.

If all the students in the class made their list of their favorite ten books, the teacher could also tabulate the ten overall favorite books for the class. Students are fascinated to know what each other's favorite books were and what the overall top ten books of the class turned out to be.

This is also a great way for teachers to assess the incoming class' interests and experiences in reading and to prepare for their arrival by adding some appropriate books to the classroom library.

REPORT CARDS

It is very difficult to construct a report card that would be applicable to all schools, but we have given two samples that may serve as a base for teachers to work from when they are planning a report card that would be appropriate for their school.

#1   **GRADES 1 AND 2**
          SAMPLE LANGUAGE ARTS REPORT

Date _____

Name _____ Room _____ Teacher _____

REPORTING KEY

1. Not yet apparent   This behavior has not yet been observed by the teacher.
2. Emerging   The child has been observed to occasionally attempt this behavior.
3. Focus of learning   The child will often attempt and show interest in this behavior, experimenting with correct usage.
4. Used effectively   "Effective" means using the behavior correctly to get
    and efficiently   things done. "Efficient" means that the behavior is performed without undue effort.

This report is to be used where possible in conjunction with children's work samples, a parent observation questionnaire, and a teacher/student/parent child evaluation conference.

A. READING BEHAVIORS OF CHILD	Not Yet Apparent	Emerging	Focus of Learning	Uses Effectively and Efficiently
1) Displays book handling skills	☐	☐	☐	☐
2) Enjoys being read to	☐	☐	☐	☐
3) Enjoys reading books	☐	☐	☐	☐
4) Frequently reads books	☐	☐	☐	☐
5) Uses reading skills to predict what will happen next in a story	☐	☐	☐	☐
6) What the child reads (orally) makes sense	☐	☐	☐	☐
7) What the child reads (orally) sounds like language	☐	☐	☐	☐
8) Can read orally with expression and meaning	☐	☐	☐	☐
9) Reads independently	☐	☐	☐	☐

Additional Comments _____

_____

_____

_____

B. WRITING BEHAVIORS OF CHILD	Not Yet Apparent	Emerging	Focus of Learning	Uses Effectively and Efficiently
1) Is willing to write	☐	☐	☐	☐
2) Writes on a variety of topics	☐	☐	☐	☐
3) Writes in a variety of genres	☐	☐	☐	☐
4) Demonstrates awareness of audience	☐	☐	☐	☐
5) Writes for a variety of purposes	☐	☐	☐	☐
6) Is willing to revise	☐	☐	☐	☐
7) Writing demonstrates voice	☐	☐	☐	☐
8) Gathers appropriate information before writing	☐	☐	☐	☐
9) Shows developed editing skills	☐	☐	☐	☐

Additional Comments _____

_____

_____

_____

C. SPELLING BEHAVIORS OF CHILD	Not Yet Apparent	Emerging	Focus of Learning	Uses Effectively and Efficiently
1) Uses functional spelling where appropriate	☐	☐	☐	☐
2) Shows an interest in learning about spelling	☐	☐	☐	☐
3) Spelling approximations are moving toward standard spelling	☐	☐	☐	☐

Additional Comments _____

_____

_____

_____

N.B.   The items above are a sample list and should be altered to meet the specific needs of each school.

#2   SAMPLE LANGUAGE ARTS REPORT (Anecdotal)

Name _____ Room _____

Teacher _____ Date _____

READING

Inventory: *This would include such things as the number of books read, the number of pages read, favorite authors or illustrators, and topics or genres read frequently. This information comes mainly from the bulk reading form.*

Use of the Reading Process:

This section can indicate such things as; the child's ability to predict; use of the cuing systems in balance; constructing text that makes sense and sounds like language; reading in chunks of meaning and at an appropriate rate; and use of a variety of strategies when encountering unknown words. This information comes mainly from the Reading Development Continuum placements and the reading observation card used to record information when the child reads orally to a teacher.

WRITING

Inventory: *This would include the number of pieces started, the number brought to publication stage, topics the child writes on, and the different genres used by the child. This information would come from the child's writing folder, portfolio, and other finished pieces.*

Use of the Writing Process:

This would include discussion of how the child gathers information and aligns information before writing and his/her strategies for drafting, revising, editing, and bringing pieces to published form. The teacher's writing observation card is the main source of this information.

Writing for Different Purposes:

This would be a comment on the different purposes the student is using writing for. Purpose always drives the process and product. The child's finished pieces and casual writings (notes and reminders) will provide information regarding the child's purposes for writing.

SPELLING

This would include an explanation of the child's stage in spelling development (the main hypothesis about spelling the child displays in his/her writing). This information comes from the Spelling Placement form. N.B. Written samples of the child's writing, and the spelling miscues generated in that writing, are essential for use during discussions with parents.

Spelling Growth:

This is best shown to parents by illustrating the child's growth in spelling toward the standard, as shown on the child's Progressive Approximation form. In upper grades (5-9), the focus begins to shift to the child's use and understanding of syntactic and semantic spelling information.

Parents are, and have a right to be, concerned about their child's overall growth in Language Arts. They need to know one of the following descriptions regarding their child:

1. The child consistently exceeds expectations for his/her level and needs to be challenged with individualized projects and materials.
2. The child consistently meets expectations for his/her level and is progressing well toward greater literacy.
3. The child is not consistently meeting expectations for his/her level but is making progress toward greater literacy.
4. The child is not consistently meeting expectations for his/her level and little progress toward greater literacy is occurring.

N.B. In a well-written anecdotal report card, you can tell which student is being evaluated without looking at the name on the report because each comment is personal and unique to the individual child.

Some Final Reminders on Reporting to Parents

Report cards and *teacher/student/parent* conferences often create stress for everyone involved. Teachers feel anxious as they try to assess the students work honestly and accurately. Students feel stress as they assess their efforts. Possibly parents feel the most apprehensive. They love their children dearly and so much want them to do well. Often they feel helpless as to what they can do to help their child do better.

Because it is important for everyone to feel comfortable with the evaluation process, teachers should be cognizant of the following reminders:

1. *Build a bond with parents.* It is important that the child sees that the teacher and the parents are a team and that they are working together to help ensure his/her success in school. Parents should be invited to give suggestions. Let's always remember they know their child well.

2. *Talk about the child's strengths.* Report cards and conferences should emphasize the strengths of the child's learning and should focus on the achievements. These strengths and achievements form the basis for new learning. There is very little gain to be had from dwelling on what has not been achieved. It is also important to have samples of the student's work close at hand in order to highlight important points.

3. *Plan for the future.* This is the time to look at the direction of the learning for the next term and should involve input from the student, the parents, and the teacher.

4. *Honesty.* It is so important that the evaluation process be an honest one on the part of the student, the parent, and the teacher. If the focus of the evaluation is on strengths and achievements and on future learning, honesty becomes easier.

5. *Keep the lines of communication open.* The teacher, parent, and student should be invited and reminded to keep in close contact so the student's progress can be monitored carefully.

N.B. A final note: The ability of an individual to learn should never be in question or in doubt. We must remember that humans have an endless ability to learn and that many factors can further learning and many others can hinder it. Belief and trust in a child's ability to learn is critical and at no time should we communicate that this belief and trust are somehow in jeopardy. *Evaluation should empower and motivate the learner.*

The Teacher's Role in Whole Language Evaluation

"No one else is going to do it for us," says Norma Mickelson of Victoria, Canada. If we want meaningful whole language evaluation, it must stem from the classroom.

The Role of the Experts

Whole language evaluation is not just another form of testing. We look at the whole child over time and look at the process as well as the product of a child's learning. We cannot produce a single "whole language" test to measure children's learning.

We are all sometimes afraid that if children do not measure up on a test or meet a "norm" they are not successful learners. When we first abandoned the basals many years ago and began using good literature and having children write on a daily basis, we were afraid we might miss something children needed to learn. We didn't know what that "something" might be, but we didn't quite believe we could know enough to successfully facilitate children's learning on our own. One young teacher was particularly agitated over the question "Are they really learning?" One day, we gave her class a unit test from a basal series. Some of her children were "below norm," most were "at norm," and some were "above norm." The teacher felt much better about her teaching. The validity of the test was questionable, but at least some source outside of the teacher had confirmed that the children were learning. She felt better. It is hard to have the courage to develop our own classroom evaluation system and believe in it. It is a hard but necessary step for the teachers to be in charge of their own evaluation systems.

Experts Can be Blinded by the Sense of Legitimacy of a Test

A learning ''expert'' recommended, after looking at the results of a WISC-R test on a child new to a school, that the child be considered for placement in a ''special education'' class. The test had been given by another professional; the ''expert'' had never spoken to or even met the child, or contacted the child's family, and had never visited the ''special education'' class being considered for this student. The WISC-R test had become the essence of the child. All too often, the child is reduced to being a number on a paper that governs the child's future education opportunities.

Teacher-Made Marks

At times, teachers render students down to a mark that they have devised. A very successful junior high teacher that I know almost never made it into the university education program. His grade twelve geography mark was too low for the entrance standards and his teacher didn't want to raise the mark. Fortunately, this teacher had a vice-principal who had a less punitive view of education and raised the geography mark to the necessary level. The teacher went successfully through university and into a teaching career. How fortunate that his geography mark did not bar the door of educational opportunity for this teacher.

Factors to Consider in Designing Your Classroom Whole Language Evaluation System

1. *Evaluation should be inclusive.*

Its goal should be to open doors to educational opportunities for the child rather than closing them. It should be a record of the child's strengths and abilities rather than a record of his/her failures and the things he/she cannot do. The original Binet test of intelligence was designed to exclude children from going on to higher education in France. Our evaluation must be designed to enhance, not hinder, the child's educational opportunities.

2. *Evaluation must be multifaceted.*

Whole language must look at the child in as many different ways as possible. Contributing to the child's evaluation should be many of the following:
- the child
- the parents
- the child's daily work
- the teacher talking to and listening to the child read and talk
- observation during writing and other activities
- observation of the child in group learning situations
- audiotapes
- videotapes
- project work
- other educators' observations of the child

3. *Evaluation should be observational.*

It needs to be based on what the child is actually doing and how he/she does that activity. Piaget and Vygotsky, in learning about how children learn, observed a few children intensely over time. Traditional psychology has tended to look at populations or groups of children and place their actions on bell curves. The individual child disappeared except when measured against norms for the population. The uniqueness of each child, as demonstrated by his/her observable, not comparative, behavior, is needed in whole language evaluation. Evaluation needs to be personal, not comparative.

4. *Evaluation must center on growth.*

In comparing populations, tests are used that provide a comparable "frozen moment in time" for each child. Whole language evaluation looks at the developmental nature of a child's learning. Where a child begins in his/her learning, how he/she learns, and the purpose and motivation behind the learning are equally as important as the products the child produces on a given day.

5. *Evaluation should build a child's confidence.*

When children are being evaluated and when that evaluation is shared and related to them, it should help them conceptualize what they can do and where their strengths are. It should also clarify for them the things they are in the process of learning and give them the confidence and motivation to risk new learning events.

6. *Children should be participants in evaluation.*

Children need to become self-evaluating in their reading, writing, spelling, and all use of language skills. Children should be involved in their own evaluation and should be invited to add information as to how they think their learning is going.

7. *Parents should be participants in evaluation.*
Parents, too, have information about their child's learning that can be highly valuable to the teacher. Parent-teacher interviews need to be two-way and allow parents to have input into the evaluation of their child's learning. Communicating with parents about the evaluation system of the classroom is vital. Sharing ''how'' the child's learning is being evaluated is as vital as sharing the evaluation of the child's learning.

Evaluation, the Challenge

I have never known a person who would actively pursue failure. In my experience, I have found that people tend to participate in activities where they find success. Good bowlers like to bowl, good chess players like to play chess and poor bowlers often dislike bowling and poor chess players seldom play chess.

Part of the reason that a bowler bowls well, or a chess player plays good chess is that they spend a lot of time bowling or playing chess. We do the things we find success with and we avoid the things where we encounter failure. That is probably the reason why few of us willingly major in mathematics in uiversity if we were ''D'' math students in high school.

Old style evaluation was used to screen out people from pursuing learning in certain directions. And it would. Failure discouraged and demoralized people and kept them from specific areas of learning. Unforunately failure never stays neatly contained in one area. If I fail at one or two sports and find that failure very painful, I *may* abandon pursuit of all sporting activities and come to view myself as ''unathletic.'' And that label becomes a part of who I am.

I was a poor speller. I received a mark of -80% on a grade six spelling exam. Part of who I was for many years was ''a poor speller.'' Today I am a speller. I spell as well as or better than the average adult, thanks to a university history professor who aroused my curiosity about the meaning of word parts (roots, prefixes and suffixes).

The kind of evaluation, that lessens our belief in ourselves and makes us view ourselves as ''non-learners'' in specific areas, has done more harm to students in schools that any other educational practice expect failure and permanent ability groupings. This negative evaluation is unfortunately very easy to accomplish, just write

"E" or failure on a child's work or report card.

Positive evaluation which leads to learning growth for a student, and to increased "risk" taking on the part of a student is far more difficult. Positive evaluation must be honest and build on a child's strengths. The evaluation must be done over time and noting development. It must be many faceted taking in many views of teachers, children, parents, product and process. By now I'm sure that this theme of positive evaluation and what it consists of is getting monotonous in this book. That is what whole language is all about, evaluation that is positive and leads to future learning. That is the simple test to see if an evaluation procedure fits the test of being "whole language evaluation." Now it is up to you, dear teacher, to construct your classroom evaluation system, one which will foster growth in your students learning. You can and must succeed, for the children's sake.

BIBLIOGRAPHY

Atwell, Nancie. *In the Middle.* Portsmouth N.H., Boynton Cook Publishers, 1987.

Britton, James. *Language and Learning.* Middlesex England, Penguin Books Ltd., 1970.

Buchanan, Ethel, Editor. *For the Love of Reading.* Winnipeg Canada C.E.L. Group Inc., 1986.

Buchanan, Ethel. *Spelling For Whole Language Classrooms.* Winnipeg, Whole Language Consultants Ltd., 1989.

Calkins, Lucy McCormick. *Lessons from a Child.* Portsmouth N.H., Heinemann Educational Books, Inc., 1983.

Calkins, Lucy McCormick. *The Art of Teaching Writing.* Portsmouth N.H., Heinemann Educational Books, Inc., 1986.

Clark, Margaret M. *Young Fluent Readers.* London England, Heinemann Educational Books, Inc., 1976.

Clay, Marie M. *Observing Young Readers.* Portsmouth N.H., Heinemann Educational Books, Inc., 1982.

Cochrane, Orin, Donna Cochrane, Sharen Scalena, and Ethel Buchanan. *Reading, Writing and Caring.* Winnipeg Canada, Whole Language Consultants Ltd., 1984.

Elkind, David. *Child Development and Education.* New York, Oxford University Press, 1976.

Farr, Roger and Robert F. Carey. *Reading: What Can be Measured?* Newark, International Reading Association, 1986.

Glasser, William, M.D. *Schools Without Failure.* New York, Harper Colophon Books, Harper & Row, Publishers, Inc., 1969.

Goodman, Kenneth S., Yetta M. Goodman and Wendy J. Hood. *The Whole Language Evaluation Book.* Portsmouth N.H., Heinemann Educational Books, Inc., 1989.

Goodman, Yetta, Dorothy J. Watson, and Carolyn L. Burke. *Reading Miscue Inventory.* New York, Richard C. Owens Publishers Inc., 1987.

Graves, Donald H. *Writing: Teachers and Children at Work.* Portsmouth N.H., Heinemann Educational Books, Inc., 1983.

Graves, Donald H. *Discover Your Own Literacy.* Portsmouth N.H., Heinemann Educational Books, Inc., 1990.

Mickelson, Norma I. *Evaluation in Whole Language.* University of Victoria British Columbia, Canada, Centre for Whole Language, n.d.

Murray, Donald M. *Expecting the Unexpected.* Portsmouth N.H., Boynton/Cook Publishers, 1989.

Newman, Judith M. *Whole Language Theory in Use.* Portsmouth N.H., Heinemann Educational Books,Inc., 1985.

Newkirk, Thomas and Nancie Atwell. *Understanding Writing.* Portsmouth N.H., Heinemann Educational Books,Inc., 1988.

Purkey, William W. *Self-Concept and School Achievement.* Englewood Cliff N.J., Prentice-Hall Inc., 1970.

Romano, Thomas. *Clearing The Way.* Portsmouth N.H., Heinemann Educational Books, Inc., 1987.

Sigel, Irving E., and Rodney R. Cocking. *Cognitive Development from Childhood to Adolescence: A Constructive Perspective.* New York, Holt, Rinehart and Winston, 1977.

Singer, Harry, and Robert B. Ruddell. *Theoretical Models and Processes of Reading.* Newark, International Reading Association Inc., 1985.

Smith, Frank. *Reading without Nonsense.* New York, Teachers College Press, 1978.

Smith, Frank. *Understanding Reading, 2d ed.* New Jersey, Lawrence Erlbaum Associates, Inc., 1986.

Smith, Frank. *Insult to Intelligence.* New York, Arbor House Publishing Company, 1986.

Smith, Frank. *Joining the Literacy Club.* Portsmouth N.H., Heinemann Educational Books, Inc., 1988.

Turbill, Jan. *No Better Way to Teach Writing!* Portsmouth N.H., Heinemann Educational Books, Inc., 1982.

Vygotsky, Leo. Edited by Alex Kozulin. *Thought and Language.* Cambridge MA, The MIT Press, 1986.

Vygotsky, L.S. Edited by Michael Cole, Vera John-Steiner, Sylvia Scribner, and Ellen Soubeerman. *Mind in Society.* Cambridge MA, Harvard University Press, 1978.

Weaver, Constance. *Reading Process and Practice.* Portsmouth N.H., Heinemann Educational Books, Inc., 1988.

Weaver, Constance. *Understanding Whole Language.* Portsmouth N.H., Heinemann Educational Books, Inc., 1990.

Wells, Gordon. *The Meaning Makers.* Portsmouth N.H., Heinemann Educational Books, Inc., 1986.

Blackline Masters

R.D.C. PAGE 1   N.B. Use different color ink for each date's observation

Grade _____

Teacher _____

Date _____

Date _____

Date _____

Date _____

NAME	MAGICAL		SELF-CONCEPTOR				BRIDGING				TAKE-OFF		INDEPENDENT			
	M1	M2	SC1	SC2	SC3	SC4	B1	B2	B3	B4	TO1	TO2	I1	I2	I3	I4

R.D.C. PAGE 2   N.B. Use different color ink for each date's observation

	SKILLED				ADVANCE SKILLED											
NAME	INFORMATION	ENTERTAINMENT	READ TO READ	MAINTENANCE OF SELF	NARRATIVE	POETRY	TV GUIDES	GRAPHS	MAPS	ENCYCLOPEDIA RESEARCH	HISTORICAL	MAGAZINES	CATALOGUES	TELEPHONE BOOKS		

Grade _____

Teacher _____

Date _____

Date _____

Date _____

Date _____

R.D.C. PAGE 3   N.B. Use different color ink for each date's observation

Grade _____

Teacher _____

Date _____

Date _____

Date _____

Date _____

NAME	Grapho-Phonic Transparent				Grapho-Phonic Fixated				Disinterest				ESL Reader		ESL Non Reader	
	1	2	3	4	1	2	3	4	1	2	3	4	1	2	1	2

Level 1 indicates highest degree of difficulty for the child.

**BULK READING
RECORD SHEET**

GRADE _____ ROOM _____

NAME _____

SHEET NUMBER _____

	TITLE	AUTHOR	PAGES	DATE COMPLETED	FOLLOW UP
1.					
2.					
3.					
4.					
5.					
6.					
7.					
8.					
9.					
10.					
		TOTAL			

Student's Reflections: _____

_____

_____

Reading Plan: _____

_____

_____

Teacher's Comments: _____

_____

_____

	EPISODE #I	EPISODE #II	EPISODE #III
Setting Who			
When			
Where			
What			
Initiating Event or Problem			
Internal Reaction Emotion			
Plan			
External Reaction or Attempt			
Outcome			
Ending			
TOTAL 100 TEACHER REFLECTIONS		Score _____	

Writing Interview — In order to get further insights into the student's view of writing, the following interview might be given.

WRITING INTERVIEW

Name _____ Age _____ Grade _____

This interview is to gather information about writing as a construction-of-meaning process.

1. How do you pick a topic to write about?_____

_____

_____

2. How do you gather information in order to get ready for writing? _____

_____

_____

3. How do you ensure a good beginning for your piece?_____

_____

_____

4. What do you do when you are writing and you don't know what to say next? _____

_____

_____

5. What do you do if you have a problem of what to write in the next piece? _____

_____

_____

6. Who do you know who is a good writer? What do you like about that person's writing? _____

_____

_____

7. What do you like about your writing? _____

_____

_____

8. What would you like to improve in your writing or in what you write? _____

_____

_____

9. What would you say is the easiest thing about writing? _____

_____

_____

10. What would you say is the most difficult thing about writing?

_____

_____

_____

11. Are you a good writer? How do you know? _____

_____

_____

12. If you were to teach someone how to write, what are some things you would say that you think would be helpful to that learner? _____

_____

_____

Pre-Phonetic Spelling Placement Form

1. Have the student write his/her own name at the top of the page.
2. Then have the student write a sentence like this.

    I live with my mom and dad in a beautiful house.

Observations:

    a) Is the child's name spelled correctly?

    b) Does the child use only letters to spell words?

    c) Are *mom* and *dad* spelled with the same number of symbols?

    d) Does the child use one or more symbols per word?

    e) Does *beautiful* have more than one symbol?

    f) Is there more than one symbol per syllable?

    g) Does the child have the correct beginning letter for *mom*, *dad*, and *beautiful?*

    h) Does the child have the correct beginning letter for *with* or *house?*

SPELLING PLACEMENT TEST

1. me	1. no	1. so
2. dog	2. dig	2. dad
3. mat	3. man	3. mop
4. rat	4. run	4. rag
5. bad	5. bag	5. big
6. name	6. nap	6. not
7. top	7. tip	7. tin
8. pot	8. pat	8. pan
9. frog	9. fat	9. free
10. kiss	10. keep	10. kit
11. pet	11. set	11. met
12. sit	12. pit	12. fit
13. fat	13. bat	13. rat
14. goat	14. game	14. go
15. cat	15. call	15. come
16. hit	16. help	16. home
17. watch	17. water	17. wand
18. jump	18. bump	18. pump
19. the	19. is	19. was
20. bar	20. car	20. far
21. hate	21. spade	21. shade
22. my	22. try	22. sky
23. toy	23. boy	23. joy
24. now	24. cow	24. bow
25. green	25. seen	25. teen
26. tick	26. truck	26. puck
27. skate	27. slice	27. slime
28. walking	28. talking	28. pulling
29. coat	29. boat	29. toad
30. when	30. where	30. why
31. stand	31. still	31. stamp
32. they	32. because	32. does
33. boot	33. toot	33. root
34. jolly	34. funny	34. pretty

SPELLING PLACEMENT TEST

35. drape	35. dress	35. drip
36. dew	36. flew	36. stew
37. work	37. worth	37. worm
38. giant	38. germ	38. gentle
39. right	39. light	39. fight
40. quiet	40. queen	40. quit
41. steam	41. leaf	41. mean
42. making	42. riding	42. hiding
43. running	43. winning	43. shopping
44. found	44. sound	44. round
45. coin	45. oil	45 soil
46. nation	46. station	46. fraction
47. enough	47. tough	47. rough
48. knee	48. knock	48. wrong
49. manage	49. garbage	49. cabbage
50. church	50. chicken	50. children
51. crafts	51. bomb	51. sign
52. worked	52. walked	52. talked
53. wanted	53. started	53. sounded
54. northerly	54. elderly	54. easterly
55. childish	55. foolish	55. whitish
56. survey	56. surmount	56. surname
57. happier	57. prettier	57. funnier
58. recall	58. regain	58. remember
59. contrary	59. contraband	59. contradict
60. Spain	60. England	60. France
61. girl's	61. boy's	61. cat's
62. boys'	62. girls'	62. dogs'
63. national	63. natural	63. extremity
64. competition	64. explanation	64. inclination
65. medicine	65. revision	65. gradual
66. dishonest	66. dishonour	66. disgust
67. irresistible	67. irregular	67. irrational
68. predict	68. prefer	68. predate

SPELLING PLACEMENT TEST

69. death	69. health	69. breadth
70. company	70. fallacy	70. truancy
71. sorrowful	71. hopeful	71. mournful
72. redness	72. fullness	72. greatness
73. children's	73. mice's	73. oxen's
74. peerless	74. fearless	74. painless
75. obstruct	75. observe	75. obstacle
76. submit	76. subside	76. subsoil
77. violinist	77. flutist	77. receptionist
78. transmit	78. transport	78. transgress
79. civilize	79. colonize	79. economize
80. conception	80. perception	80. deception
81. gesture	81. creature	81. picture
82. unnecessary	82. unnatural	82. unnoticed
83. identical	83. historical	83. topical
84. philosopher	84. phonograph	84. telephone
85. authoress	85. giantess	85. lioness
86. pleasure	86. photography	86. introduction
87. illegal	87. irregular	87. illiterate
88. biology	88. sociology	88. criminology
89. toxic	89. dramatic	89. mimic
90. docile	90. fragile	90. tactile
91. homicide	91. suicide	91. genocide
92. sympathy	92. syllable	92. symmetry
93. atheism	93. barbarism	93. organism
94. mathematics	94. ethics	94. graphics
95. uncomplaining	95. uncommitted	95. uncomfortable
96. predictable	96. predetermined	96. precise
97. polygon	97. polygraph	97. polyester
98. foreshadow	98. foreground	98. foretell
99. studious	99. melodious	99. odious
100. exonerate	100. exquisite	100. exorbitant

SPELLING MISCUE OBSERVATION

Student Name _____   Room _____

Observation Date _____

Miscue #	Text Item #	TEXT	SCRIPT	OBSERVATION
1.				
2.				
3.				
4.				
5.				
6.				
7.				
8.				
9.				
10.				

Conclusion
(reflection, spelling stage) _____

_____

_____

_____

_____

Progressive Approximation Form

FORM B

% OF SPELLING MISCUES MOVING TOWARD STANDARD SPELLING

Student Name _____   Room _____

Observation Dates: 1st_____

2nd_____

	TEXT	SCRIPT 1	SCRIPT 2	SYMBOL
1.				
2.				
3.				
4.				
5.				
6.				
7.				
8.				
9.				
10.				

KEY TO SYMBOLS: + = moving toward standard spelling
                  N = no change
                  – = moving away from standard spelling

Number of +'s = __.

__/10 x 100 = __%

__% of the child's miscues are moving toward, or have become, standard spelling.

CLASS SUMMARY OF
SPELLING MISCUE OBSERVATIONS
NB   Use different color ink to record each date's observations.

Teacher _____

Date _____

Date _____

Date _____

Date _____

	Pre-Phonetic				Early Phonetic			Advanced Phonetic			Phonic			Syntactic -Semantic	
	Not yet apparent	Emerging	Dominant Strategy	Remains partially in use	Emerging	Dominant Strategy	Remains partially in use	Emerging	Dominant Strategy	Remains partially in use	Emerging	Dominant Strategy	Remains partially in use	Emerging	Dominant Strategy

Parent's Observation Form

		Mon.	Tues.	Wed.	Thurs.	Fri.	Week end
I	Time spent at home:						
	Reading to my child						
	My child reading to me						
	My child reading to himself/herself						
	TOTAL						

II   My child's favorite book for me to read to him/her: _____

_____

III   Approximate number of times a week my child will write something at home:___

_____

My child uses writing (e.g. to write thank you notes, telephone messages, letters to

friends and relatives, stories, etc.):_____

_____

IV   Three things my child likes to do at home: Please elaborate.

1. _____

2. _____

3 _____

V   Topics my child is very interested in: _____

_____

_____

VI   My child feels this way about reading and writing: _____

_____

_____

VII   My child tells me he/she likes to do this in school: _____

_____

_____

VIII I feel the school does this well: _____

_____

_____

IX   I would like to know more about: _____

_____

_____

Student Resumé for Elementary School Students

Student Name _____

School _____

Grade _____ **Room** _____ **Date** _____

Birthdate: Month _____ **Day** _____ **Year** _____

The best thing I ever did in school was _____

_____

_____

_____

_____

I am _____

_____

_____

_____

_____

I like _____

_____

_____

_____

_____

I don't like _____

_____

_____

_____

My family _____

_____

_____

_____

I would like to learn next year _____

_____

_____

_____

FORM I

_____

Student's Signature

Student Resumé for Going into Junior High

Student Name _____

Elementary School _____

Date _____

Birthdate: Month _____ Day _____ Year _____

Background Information (birthplace, family members) _____

_____

_____

_____

Elementary Career (interests, strengths, weaknesses) _____

_____

_____

_____

Personality (strengths, weaknesses) _____

_____

_____

_____

_____

Personal Goals (short term and long term) _____

_____

_____

_____

_____

Questions and Concerns about Junior High _____

_____

_____

_____

_____

Expectations of Junior High _____

_____

_____

_____

FORM 2

_____

Student's Signature

#1

GRADES 1 AND 2
SAMPLE LANGUAGE ARTS REPORT

Date _____

Name _____ Room _____ Teacher _____

REPORTING KEY

1. Not yet apparent — This behavior has not yet been observed by the teacher.
2. Emerging — The child has been observed to occasionally attempt this behavior.
3. Focus of learning — The child will often attempt and show interest in this behavior, experimenting with correct usage.
4. Used effectively and efficiently — "Effective" means using the behavior correctly to get things done. "Efficient" means that the behavior is performed without undue effort.

This report is to be used where possible in conjunction with children's work samples, a parent observation questionnaire, and a teacher/student/parent child evaluation conference.

A. READING BEHAVIORS OF CHILD	Not Yet Apparent	Emerging	Focus of Learning	Uses Effectively and Efficiently
1) Displays book handling skills	☐	☐	☐	☐
2) Enjoys being read to	☐	☐	☐	☐
3) Enjoys reading books	☐	☐	☐	☐
4) Frequently reads books	☐	☐	☐	☐
5) Uses reading skills to predict what will happen next in a story	☐	☐	☐	☐
6) What the child reads (orally) makes sense	☐	☐	☐	☐
7) What the child reads (orally) sounds like language	☐	☐	☐	☐
8) Can read orally with expression and meaning	☐	☐	☐	☐
9) Reads independently	☐	☐	☐	☐

Additional Comments _____

_____

_____

_____

B. WRITING BEHAVIORS OF CHILD	Not Yet Apparent	Emerging	Focus of Learning	Uses Effectively and Efficiently
1) Is willing to write	☐	☐	☐	☐
2) Writes on a variety of topics	☐	☐	☐	☐
3) Writes in a variety of genres	☐	☐	☐	☐
4) Demonstrates awareness of audience	☐	☐	☐	☐
5) Writes for a variety of purposes	☐	☐	☐	☐
6) Is willing to revise	☐	☐	☐	☐
7) Writing demonstrates voice	☐	☐	☐	☐
8) Gathers appropriate information before writing	☐	☐	☐	☐
9) Shows developed editing skills	☐	☐	☐	☐

Additional Comments _____

_____

_____

_____

C. SPELLING BEHAVIORS OF CHILD	Not Yet Apparent	Emerging	Focus of Learning	Uses Effectively and Efficiently
1) Uses functional spelling where appropriate	☐	☐	☐	☐
2) Shows an interest in learning about spelling	☐	☐	☐	☐
3) Spelling approximations are moving toward standard spelling	☐	☐	☐	☐

Additional Comments _____

_____

_____

_____

N.B.   The items above are a sample list and should be altered to meet the specific needs of each school.